Christmas 1987
To Daddy
from Sam
with love + o + o

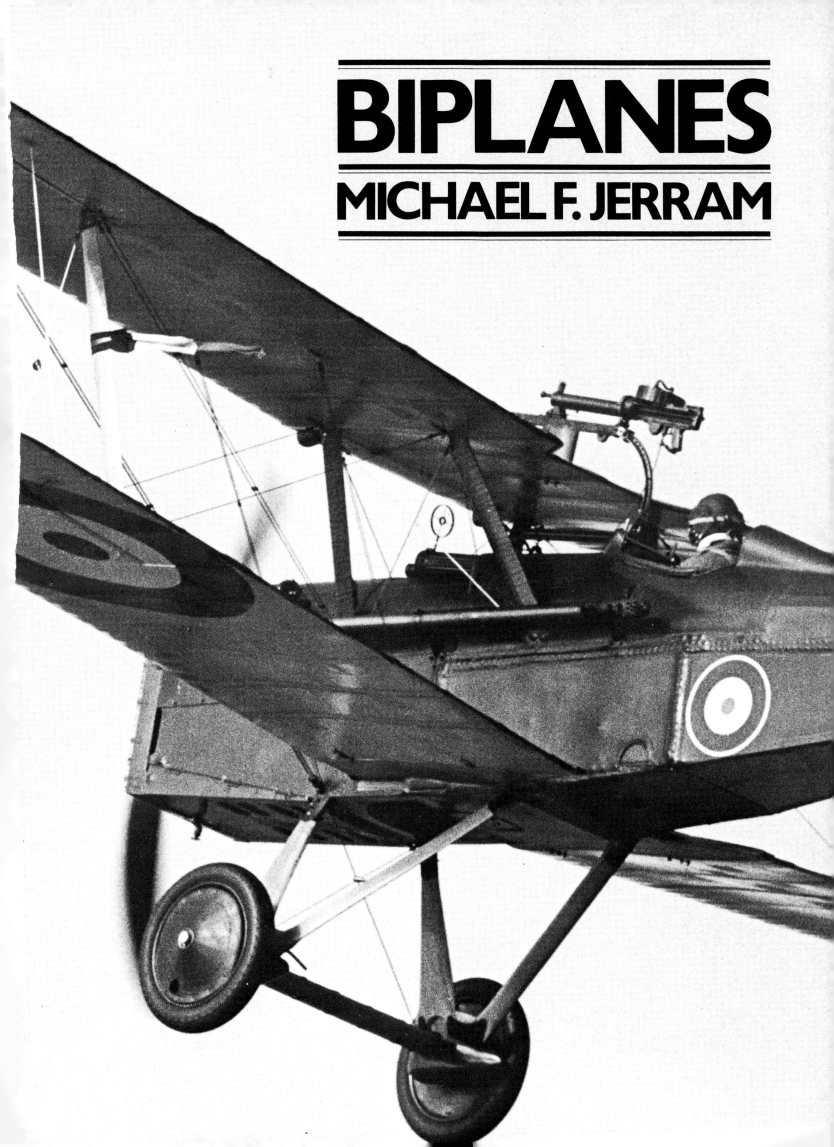

BIPLANES
MICHAEL F. JERRAM

BIPLANES
MICHAEL F. JERRAM

MICHAEL JOSEPH
LONDON

First published in Great Britain by
Michael Joseph Ltd
44 Bedford Square, London WC1
1982

ISBN 0 7181 2151 1

Produced by
Winchmore Publishing
Services Ltd.,
48 Lancaster Avenue,
Hadley Wood, Herts.

Designed by
Laurence Bradbury
Design assistant: Fiona Barlow
Edited by Sue Butterworth

Printed in Hong Kong

CONTENTS

PREFACE

Biplane: an aeroplane having two mainplane surfaces, set one above the other.

Thus, in cold unfeeling terms my dictionary defines a word which seldom fails to evoke a pang of unashamed nostalgia wherever men or women fly, even among those who cannot remember when all aeroplanes had 'two mainplane surfaces set one above the other'.

Why biplanes? There is no precedent in nature, for you will find no biplane birds – though the dragonfly comes close. It just happened that in the early days of flight the truss-rigged biplane arrangement provided an easy means of building a strong yet light structure, which survived almost unchallenged for several decades. Still *does* survive, for biplanes are being built in the 1980s for special purposes for which no better configuration has been found. There never was a biplane era; it is still with us.

The great biplanes described and illustrated in these pages are, of necessity, a personal and subjective selection from 80 years of biplane flight. If I have omitted your special favourite, I can only hope that something here will capture for you the spirit of those wings and wires, the glint of sunlight on the fabric stitching of a wing, and (yes, why not?) the *romance* of feeling wind on cheek and seeing the world between those two sets of mainplanes.

Mike Jerram, Southsea, Hampshire,
January 1982.

THE WRIGHTS

Eight hundred and fifty-two feet. About three hundred paces for a man. That was the modest distance covered by Orville Wright on 17 December 1903, the longest of four flights made that day and the one which lives in history as man's first powered, controlled flight.

The Wrights, bicycle makers from Dayton, Ohio, had been infatuated with the notion of mechanical flight from childhood. In 1899 Wilbur wrote to Professor Samuel P. Langley, director of the prestigious Smithsonian Institution in Washington, D.C., confiding in him that he was an 'addict of mechanical flight' and was convinced that it was possible for a human being to fly. 'I am an enthusiast, but not a crank,' he assured Langley. There followed several years of

A Wright biplane rounding a marker pylon at Rheims during the Grand Semaine d'Aviation in 1909.

thorough and systematic research, during which the two Wright boys studied every available paper on the experimenters – both serious and fatuous – who had gone before them. Their approach was scientific, meticulous, yet fired with the zeal of the amateur. They built a wind-tunnel to evaluate wing airfoil sections, and used the knowledge gained to construct a series of biplane gliders which they flew as tethered kites and in free flight from Big Kill Devil Hill at Kitty Hawk, North Carolina in the first years of the twentieth century.

The most important discovery which the Wright Brothers made during those years was the need to *control* their flying machines. Many of the early experimenters assumed that their aeroplanes would have natural stability. The Wrights had no such delusions. Very early in their trials they introduced warping wings on their gliders to provide lateral control by means of a rocking cradle arrangement on which the pilot lay on top of the lower wing, the prone position was chosen to lessen the wind resistance of the pilot's body.

By the autumn of 1902 the Wrights had perfected their glider design and made nearly 1,000 flights in an intensive 39-day testing period during which they succeeded in travelling a maximum of 622 feet above the sands at Kitty Hawk. In addition to wing-warping they incorporated a forward 'rudder', which we would now term an elevator or canard surface, and a rear-mounted vertical stabiliser to counter the machines' tendency to slide sideways into the ground when making a turn. Control in all three axes – roll, pitch and yaw – had thus been achieved.

One problem remained: motive power. And here the Wrights assumed, incorrectly, that the fledgling automobile industry would provide a suitable powerplant for their aeroplane. They

were surprised and disappointed to discover that early automobile engines were too heavy and produced too little power for flight, so they ran tests to determine the optimum power-to-weight ratio needed, and designed and built their own motor. It was a four-cylinder water-cooled inline with an aluminium block. And it was crude, weighing 200 pounds with fuel (just one gallon), oil and water, and producing at best around 16 hp before it overheated and dropped its power output to nearer 12 hp, just barely enough for their purpose.

The Wrights also designed their own propellers, correctly ignoring the then popular assumption that a propeller 'screwed' its way through the air, which was quite wrong, as indeed is the term 'airscrew'. What was needed was a vertical rotating wing surface with an airfoil section. The Wright's eight foot diameter propellers were remarkably efficient, converting 66 per cent torque to thrust. They used two, linked to the engine by chains (and contrary to popular myth they were *not* bicycle chains), one of which was crossed so that the propellers counter-rotated to eliminate torque effect. The pilot lay along the aircraft's centreline with the engine offset to the right both to counterbalance his weight and to ensure that it would not crush him in a crash, and the right wing panels were made four inches longer than

those on the left to compensate for the difference in weights between pilot and engine.

This, then, was the 1903 Wright Flyer on which Wilbur first attempted powered flight at Kitty Hawk on Monday 14 December 1903. Orville recalled later: 'We tossed up a coin to decide who should make the first trial and Will won. While I was signalling the man at the other end to leave go, and before I myself was ready, Will started the machine. I grabbed the upright as best I could and off we went. By the time we had reached the last quarter of the third rail the speed was so great that I could stay with it no longer.' The Flyer lifted about six or eight feet, then pitched up, rose to perhaps 15 feet, and sank back to the sand, breaking a skid and some struts but without injuring Wilbur. It had stalled. Fortuitously the brothers had built into their machines a safety device which undoubtedly saved their lives many times during their gliding experiments. By choosing the 'forward rudder' or canard, instead of a rear-mounted elevator, they had unwittingly provided the machines with an anti-stall feature, so that when the aircraft entered the stall it did not pitch down violently or enter a spin, but 'parachuted' to earth in a flat attitude which offered the pilot a good chance of survival.

Three days after Will's upset Orville made the

Aeroplanes have always provided shelter from the elements for spectators. Here a Wright machine serves as makeshift umbrella at the 1909 Rheims meeting.

first successful powered flight, a hop of no more than 12 seconds' duration, then they took turns to fly, ending the day with the historic 852-foot flight. Orville cabled his sister Katharine back home in Dayton: *Success. Four flights Thursday morning all against 21 mile wind. Started from level with engine power alone. Average speed through air 31 miles. Longest 57 seconds. Inform Press. Home Christmas.*

The Western Union telegraph company took two seconds off the Flyer's flight time in transmitting the message. Orville's exhortation to inform the Press brought a stunning silence, either from disbelief or lack of interest. Only the *Norfolk Virginian Pilot* troubled to report their achievement with a highly-coloured account of a flight over *three miles*, and equipping the Flyer with a six-blade vertical lift propeller in addition to the two which the Wrights found sufficient for flight. The lack of Press interest soured the brothers and for some five years they refused to make public any details of their aircraft or experiments in an enforced silence born more of naïveté than arrogance.

Thus when they resumed their experiments at home in Ohio in the early spring of 1904 using a new Flyer (the 1903 model never flew again after 17 December) Orville and Wilbur took pains to avoid publicity, timing their attempted flights from a field at Huffman Prairie to miss the passage of trains which ran along tracks skirting their 'airfield'. It was a fortunate decision, for the 1904 Flyer, which had a more powerful and reliable engine than the first machine, simply refused to fly at all during their earliest attempts. Wilbur attributed this failure to the 'rustiness' of

its pilots. More likely the fault lay in the location. Huffman Prairie was 815 feet above sea-level, and the daytime temperatures in spring rose to the low 80s, equivalent to a density altitude of 2,900 feet above sea-level. By contrast Kitty Hawk, the site of their many previous experiments, was at sea-level, and on 17 December the temperature had been just 34 degrees Fahrenheit, producing an effective density altitude of 1,800 feet *below* sea-level. The combination of altitude and temperature in Ohio produced thin unsupportive air (hence the reference by many early aviators to days when 'there was no lift in the air'), and also robbed the Flyer's engine of what little power it had. To compensate the brothers devised a weight-and-pulley catapult system to give the Flyer needed impetus and soon were making controlled circling flights around the field.

Although they still eschewed publicity, the successes of 1904 inspired the Wrights to offer their invention to the US Government. 'The series of aeronautical experiments upon which we have been engaged for the past five years has ended in the production of a flying machine of a type fitted for practical use. It not only flies through the air at high speed, but it also lands without being wrecked,' they wrote to their congressman. 'During the year 1904 one hundred and five flights were made . . . and though our experience in handling the machine has been too short to give any high degrees of skill we nevertheless succeeded towards the end of the season in making two flights of five minutes each, in which we sailed round and round the field until a distance of about three miles had been covered at a speed

After many years at the Science Museum in London the original Wright Flyer now takes pride of place at the National Air & Space Museum in Washington D.C.

of thirty-five miles an hour . . . If you can find it convenient to ascertain whether this subject is of interest to our own government, it would oblige us greatly, as early information on this point will aid us in making our plans for the future.' The reply was swift, and totally discouraging. The US War Department could see no practical use for aeroplanes and they turned down the Wrights' offer flat.

The Huffman Prairie experiments continued throughout 1905 with a third Flyer, this one making flights of up to 39 minutes' duration under perfect control, and is recognised as the first truly successful powered aeroplane offering total controllability. But such was the level of official apathy that in the following two years the Wrights all but gave up flying and concentrated instead on the development of their machine and its protection by patents.

It was not until 1908 that they achieved their first financial gain, when they accepted a contract to demonstrate their Flyer publicly in France, thus robbing America of the first chance to see true powered flight. (Though by this time the War Department had thought better of their earlier rejection and were canvassing bids for a

'military flying machine' capable of carrying two people at 40 mph for ten miles, and received offers of such aeroplanes for sums ranging from a modest $1,000 to an absurd $10 million. The Wrights bid at $25,000 and were among few contenders capable of delivering the goods.)

The 1908 Flyer had a new 30 hp engine, and instead of laying in the hip cradle used on earlier machines its pilot now sat upright, and had a spare seat for a passenger. The hip cradle control system was replaced by two hand levers, one for pitch control, the other for roll, though unlike a modern aircraft's control column they both moved in a fore and aft motion. When Wilbur flew the machine at Hunaudières racetrack near Le Mans at the start of his 1908 European tour he faced an audience of sceptics, for at the time European progress in powered aviation had been dismal. Paris newspapers unequivocally called the Wrights 'bluffers'. But after Wilbur's first public flight of a mere two minutes' duration a veteran French pioneer threw up his arms in surrender. 'We are beaten! We do not exist!,' he cried. Wilbur made more than one hundred public flights in France, and carried many passengers, dazzling witnesses with his total mastery of the air.

What was the significance of the Wright brothers and their Flyer? Not that they invented the aeroplane, as is often erroneously supposed. Not even that they made what is generally accepted as man's first powered flight, because that 1903 Flyer was a poor flying machine, barely controllable. What makes the Wrights so special in aviation's history is that they were the first experimenters to realise the importance of controlling their machine, not just to prevent it crashing, but to direct its flight in every axis, to make it do what they wanted so that the pilot was truly in command, not just a poor passenger on a headlong dash to destruction. That they did it with their own money, in the face of much public scepticism and ridicule, and with little owed to the work of their forerunners or contemporaries save for inspiration, qualifies the two Dayton bicycle makers for a special place in any aviation history. They were visionaries, scientists, patriots. Above all they were persistent, determined, and their self-confidence paid off in the discovery, in four years of experimentation, of a secret which for decades – centuries even – had eluded the world's greatest inventors.

Above left: Wilbur Wright flying at Pau in 1909 (and proving wrong the fear that flying machines had no military use because they would frighten cavalry horses).

Left: The Wrights' third glider being launched at Kitty Hawk in 1902.

THE FASTEST MAN ALIVE

Glenn Hammond Curtiss made his entry into the history books of aviation on a singularly appropriate day – 4 July 1908. On that day Curtiss flew his *June Bug* biplane 5,090 feet in 1 minute 42.2 seconds to win the *Scientific American* magazine's trophy for the first officially-observed flight of over one kilometre in America. Like the Wrights, Curtiss was in the business of bicycle manufacture and repair and was noted for the excellence of the engines which he developed for motor cycles, one of which earned him the title of

The World's Fastest Human Being on 24 January 1907 when he rode at the astonishing speed of 136.3 mph at Ormond Beach, Florida.

Curtiss's engines had high power/weight ratios – a commodity much sought after by early aviators. It was thus not surprising that he was approached first to build an engine for an airship, and later to join Alexander Graham Bell's Aerial Experiment Association as Director of Experiments. The *June Bug* was the most successful and best-known of the AEA's flying machines. It was not unlike the Wright Flyer in general appearance, having a single forward elevator and a box tail enclosing the rudder. Curtiss employed a 40 hp V-8 engine of his own design to drive a single pusher propeller, and fitted the

Replica Curtiss Pusher pictured at an antique aircraft fly-in in the United States.

biplane with a then revolutionary (no pun intended) tricycle undercarriage. Movable wing-tips provided roll control and led to a protracted and bitter legal action brought by the Wright brothers who alleged that Curtiss's design infringed their wing-warping patents, which they were attempting to license to other constructors for fees said to have amounted to $1,000 a day. The action was not settled for many years, when the two opposing factions merged as the Curtiss-Wright Corporation, long after the principal protagonists had departed the scene.

Although his speed through the air, at 39 mph, was barely more than one quarter that he had achieved on two wheels, Curtiss's Independence Day flight was a triumph, which he reported with great enthusiasm:

'She skimmed over the old racetrack *(at Hammondsport, New York – Curtiss's birthplace amid the wine-making region of the Finger Lakes)* for perhaps two hundred feet and then rose gracefully in the air. The crowd set up a hearty cheer, as I was told later – I could hear nothing but the roar of the motor, and I saw nothing except the course and the flag marking the distance of one kilometre. The flag was quickly reached and passed and I still kept the Aerodrome *(June Bug's official designation was Aerodrome No.3)* up . . . finally coming down safely in a meadow fully a mile from the starting place. I might have gone a good deal farther as

the motor was working beautifully and I had the machine under perfect control, but to have prolonged the flight would have meant a turn in the air or passing over a number of trees.'

While he was still working for Bell's Association Curtiss accepted a commission from the Aeronautic Society of New York to build a new aircraft, for which he would receive a sum of $5,000 to include flying instruction for two members of the Society. This machine, known variously as the Curtiss No.I, the Herring-Curtiss No.I (Curtiss formed a partnership with Augustus M. Herring of Rochester, New York, in March 1909), the Model D, and *Gold Bug*, is best remembered as the *Golden Flier*, so called because of the yellow-gold colour of its rubberised silk covering. It was the first in a range of biplanes known collectively as 'Curtiss Pushers' and was a development of the final AEA design *Silver Dart*, with new rectangular, dihedral-less wings incorporating separate 'winglet' ailerons at the mid-points of the interplane struts so as to

avoid further claims from the Wrights, whose patents applied only to warping roll controls which were integral with the wing.

The *Golden Flier*'s tail was a cruciform tailplane/rudder unit, while a biplane front elevator was installed, carried forward on bamboo poles. A contemporary journal described the machine's control system thus:

'Immediately in front of the pilot is a steering wheel, having a fore and aft motion to control the forward elevation rudder, and turning left and right to control the rear lateral rudder. The ailerons are operated by shoulder control, the seat having a light steel tube back to which the wires are attached. Natural swaying of the body corrects the balance. *(Curtiss's motor cycle experience was showing here.)* Ignition advance is obtained by means of a lever convenient to the pilot's left hand. There are three foot controls, one allowing an extra charge of oil to be pumped

Left: Glenn Hammond Curtiss.

Right: Glenn Curtiss (*rear*) apparently about to give dual instruction on a Pusher.

Below: A modern scale replica of a 'Headless' Curtiss Pusher.

to the engine as required, another short-circuiting the motor and, if pushed to its extreme limit, applying a brake to the front running wheel, while a third controls the throttle.'

In 1909 wheel brakes on aeroplanes were an innovation indeed, as was Curtiss's shoulder control, which worked well enough except that a sudden turn of the pilot's head to glance backward might induce an involuntary wing drop. Alexander Williams, one of the Aeronautic Society's designated trainee pilots, crashed the *Golden Flier* on his first attempt, breaking his left arm, which healed, and his nerve, which did not. His companion Charles Willard did succeed in teaching himself to fly the aeroplane and prompted the Herring-Curtiss sales agents to announce, with more optimism than truth: 'The operating of an aeroplane, readily handled by the amateur, is now an assured fact'. In the meantime Curtiss had built a second aeroplane, almost identical to *Golden Flier* save for slightly reduced wingspan and a new, secret 51 hp V-8 engine, with which he was to be sole American representative at the *Grand Semaine d'Aviation* at Rheims, France in August 1909 among all the most experienced European aviators.

Curtiss was to compete for a cup and $5,000 prize put up by James Gordon Bennett, proprietor of the *New York Herald* newspaper. On the seventh day of the meeting, which was blessed with near perfect weather, Curtiss and four other contestants – Blériot, Fabré and Latham from France and the Englishman Cockburn – flew around the 20-kilometre course. Curtiss completed his circuit just 40 seconds ahead of Blériot to take the Gordon Bennett Cup at an average speed of 47 mph. 'I had resolved to keep the throttle wide open,' he told reporters afterwards. 'I cut the corners as close as I dared and banked the machine high on turns. I remember I caused a great commotion among a big flock of birds which did not seem to get out of the way of the wash of my propeller. In front of the tribunes the machine flew steadily, but when I got around on the back stretch I found remarkable air conditions. There was no wind but the air seemed fairly to boil. The machine pitched considerably, and when I passed above the 'graveyard' where so many other machines had gone down and were smashed the air seemed literally to drop out from under me. It was so bad at one point that I made up my mind that if I got over safely I would avoid that particular spot thereafter.'

Later that year Curtiss decided to try for a $10,000 prize offered by the *New York World* newspaper for the first flight along the Hudson River from the state capital at Albany to New York City. In the event neither the weather nor Curtiss's new *Albany Flier* were ready until the morning of Sunday 29 May 1910, when Curtiss left Albany's Van Rensselaer Island at 7.02 am and journeyed along the Catskill Mountains to Poughkeepsie, where he refuelled, and thence to Inwood, within the NYC limits, and finally to

Governor's Island, completing the 50-mile flight at noon for a total flight time of 2 hours and 46 minutes – an average speed of 54 mph.

It was the *Albany Flier* also which made another historic flight. Foreseeing that military orders would be the key to the success of the aeroplane Curtiss began a campaign to promote his machines to the US Army and Navy, and on 14 November 1910 Eugene Ely, a member of the Curtiss Exhibition Fliers, flew the *Albany Flier* off a specially-constructed platform mounted on the forward deck of the USS *Birmingham* anchored in Hampton Roads, Virginia, the first successful flight from a ship (but only just; Ely actually hit the sea with the machine's wheels after leaving the platform). Two months later Ely landed the first Curtiss military aeroplane on the platformed aft deck of the *Pennsylvania* in San Francisco Bay, and took off again.

Modern replica of a 'Headless' Pusher. Note the bamboo structure of the fuselage.

Glenn Curtiss was fascinated with the concept of maritime aviation, having first experimented with one of the AEA machines mounted on a pair of canoes. In February 1911 (the date given is quoted variously as 17 or 26 February) he flew the world's first successful amphibian, a Pusher-derived machine called Triad, from water at North Island San Diego to a nearby sandspit, landed, took off again and made a final water landing back at his base. At this time Curtiss is also credited, erroneously, with making that classic amphibian pilot's error: landing in water

Curtiss Hydro ordered by the US Navy.

Eugene Ely making the first flight from a ship with *Albany Flier* aboard USS *Birmingham* at Hampton Roads, Virginia on 14 November 1910.

with the wheels down. In fact, while flying off water at Hammondsport one day, and planning to land on an airstrip, he found that water accumulated in the Triad's float – which was not divided into separate compartments as are those of modern seaplanes and amphibians – and sloshed forward causing the machine to go into a shallow dive which ended in the water short of his intended touch-down point.

While Curtiss's hydro experiments continued his Pusher designs were being manufactured in two main versions, the Models D and E, offered with a variety of four- and eight-cylinder powerplants in the 40-75 hp range and at prices ranging from $3,500-6,000. Two-seat versions were produced featuring a unique 'throwover' control system whereby a pilot could literally pass the control wheel over to his passenger or student, thus making true dual instruction possible. But, according to legend, the most significant change to the Curtiss Pusher came about by chance, by bad luck even. The story goes that a colourful (some might say reckless) member of the Curtiss Exhibition Fliers, called Lincoln Beachey, chanced to damage the forward elevator of his Pusher one day, and rather than lose the fee for his exhibition booking he flew anyway, without the elevator, and was surprised to find that the aeroplane actually flew better. Thus was born the archetypal 'Headless' Curtiss Pusher, which was adopted as the standard production model. Earlier aircraft were also decapitated.

Best known of the Headless Pushers was a special machine constructed in 1913 for Beachey, who was keen to become the first man to loop the loop. His *Special Looper* had a short-span wing, shorter tail outriggers and a 100 hp Curtiss OX engine. Among Beachey's accomplishments in the *Looper* was a flight *within* the Machinery Hall at San Francisco during the Panama-Pacific Exhibition. Beachey had previously used another special Pusher to set a world altitude record of 11,642 feet on 20 August 1911 and is reputed to have earned up to $4,000 a week barnstorming, stunt flying and giving car-versus-aeroplane exhibitions with great racing drivers such as Barney Oldfield and Eddie Rickenbacker. Beachey was a popular hero whose 'death dives' unfortunately inspired other aviators to copy his skilled performances. Sadly they were not to know that his Pushers were specially constructed, with doubled bracing wires, double-thickness spars and safety belts and shoulder harnesses. 'Beachey-ing' took a heavy toll among his contemporaries, and Beachey himself died at San Francisco on 14 March 1915, though not while flying a Curtiss aeroplane.

The Curtiss Pusher was one of the most significant flying machines of early American aviation, one which was (and still is) much copied. Such was Glenn Curtiss's own affection for it that he had a replica of a 1912 Pusher constructed by his company after the First World War. It is now displayed at the National Air & Space Museum in Washington, D.C.

THE PENNY NOTEBOOK PLANE

Legend has it that some of the world's most successful aeroplanes started out as doodlings on restaurant napkins or jottings on the backs of the tattered envelopes which aircraft designers are supposed to have ever at the ready for when inspiration strikes. Alliott Verdon-Roe's favoured sketchpad was a notebook, price one penny, on whose unpromising pages he first roughed out his ideas for one of the most successful biplanes of all time: the Avro 504.

In fairness, the term roughed out does scant justice to Roe's preliminary drawings which, even before he handed them over to his designers for interpretation, revealed a high standard of draughtsmanship and a very clear idea of the aeroplane he had in mind. Roe made his drawings in the spring of 1913, planning a two-seat tandem biplane with a cowled engine and a distinctive undercarriage with a long 'toothpick' skid set between the mainwheel legs. 'A piece of linen fitted on an ordinary blind roller is pulled

Left and below: The
Shuttleworth Trust's Avro
504K is the only airworthy
example in the United
Kingdom. It was originally a
Lynx-engined 504N,
modified to Avro 504K
standard during a rebuild
by A. V. Roe Company
apprentices in 1951.

over the passenger pit when no passenger (is carried)' he noted on the sketches. The wings had warping 'ailerons', whose inner ends were fixed, while the outer portions, which had increased chord, were warped for roll control.

When test pilot Fred Raynham put the prototype through its early trials at Brooklands in July 1913 he reported to Roe that the 504 had excellent handling qualities save for the warping ailerons, which offered inadequate lateral control and were soon replaced by hinged surfaces. The streamlined airframe was a masterly piece of instinctive engineering, for the design was a product of Roe's 'feel' for aeroplanes rather than any calculation, though one onlooker who watched the Avro during its many demonstration flights at Brooklands and Hendon remarked to Roe that it seemed astonishingly light. 'No,' replied Roe, not a little indignantly, 'it should

Above: Avros continued to serve with the Royal Air Force throughout the 1920s. These were photographed in the Far East.

Air Commodore Allen Wheeler flying the Shuttleworth Collection's Avro 504K at Old Warden. Note the Model T Ford-based Hucks Starter in the foreground.

rather be said that my machine is astonishingly strong for its weight. The War Office demands that certain stresses per square inch will not be exceeded. The Admiralty are more stringent, but the Avro people, to be on the safe side, keep within the Admiralty requirements.' Roe and his team had no doubts that the 504 was a winner, but in 1913 sales prospects for aeroplanes, good or bad, were not auspicious. Roe thought he might sell a half dozen. In the event he was somewhat wide of the mark, for by Armistice Day in 1918 8,340 Avro 504s had been delivered and production was set to continue until 1933 – 20 years after the first flight of the prototype – with the final total exceeding 10,000.

Despite Roe's adherence to the strictures of Admiralty specifications, when the War Office and Admiralty placed their first orders for the 504 it was the latter who demanded changes to the aircraft's structure (they wanted wing spars of greater cross-section) and no amount of arguing by Roe could persuade them differently, so he was forced to produce two different models, the Avro 504A and 504B, which were used as fighter-bombers rather than in the training role for which the aircraft had been intended. Service Avros achieved a double distinction early in the war by becoming the first British aircraft shot down and the first to drop bombs on Germany.

But it was as a trainer that the Avro left its indelible mark on history and on the minds of tens of thousands of neophyte airmen. Best known of the many 504 sub-types was the 504K which was built with a variety of rotary engines fitting a common mount. Most numerous were those powered by 100 hp Gnôme Monosoupapes; there were also 100 hp Le Rhône and 130 hp Clerget variants. A trainee pilot learning on the Avro would study his official Pilot's Notes and doubtless be pleased to learn that 'running the

engine is simple'. It was not true. Learning to minister to the needs of a cantankerous Gnôme was the hardest part of flying training. As its name implied the Monosoupape had just one valve serving as an air inlet valve and an exhaust valve in each of its seven cylinders. A tapered needle in a regulating valve provided mixture control. There was no carburettor and no throttle, and while a 'Mono' engine would respond sweetly enough to the experienced touch it would often give up when treated to the clumsy fumbling of a trainee pilot, counterpointing his flight with embarrassing silences or sudden bursts of unwanted energy.

'All set?,' an instructor would call through his Gosport Tube, a device named after the School of Special Flying established at Gosport, Hampshire by Colonel Robert Smith-Barry, the father of modern flight training. The Gosport Tube was little more than an aerial adaptation of the domestic speaking tube through which m'lord might order his after dinner brandy from below stairs. It gurgled and glugged and was just a little better than the earliest forms of inter-cockpit communication, which were mostly by thought transmission, sharp blows, a wiggle on the control stick, or, as a last resort, a scribbled note thrust into the slipstream. Up with the power, ready to correct the swing to the left with gentle pressure on the sensitive, balanced comma of a rudder. A heavy-footed student would find the Avro's nose snapping around to meet its tail and would soon be walking back to the store depot to indent for a new machine, which cost £870, less engine. Since only about four of every ten Avros built during the First World War were still on charge when the war ended it is fair to assume that A. V. Roe & Company were kept busy by the insensitive handling of tyro fliers. Or by even more experienced hands. When Avros (and other aircraft) became oil-soaked and time-weary, drained of their modest performance, it was not unknown for deliberate 'accidents' to be staged. One flying training school officer is said to have developed a perfect technique for crashing an Avro in such a way that he would emerge unscathed, but the unfortunate aeroplane would be inflicted with more than the minimum fifty per cent damage demanded by the War Office to justify replacement with a new machine rather than repair.

By the standards of its day the Avro was not a difficult machine to fly, though it suffered from poor harmonisation of its controls. The rudder was especially sensitive and demanded a delicate foot on the rudder bar. The ailerons, however, were sluggish, ineffective and provoked so much adverse yaw (the tendency for the downward-moving aileron to produce more drag than the raised surface, thus causing the aeroplane to swing in the opposition direction to the bank being applied) that a properly balanced turn needed very precise coordination – all proper and fitting for an aeroplane designed to teach people to *fly* rather than merely drive around the sky. Students were taught to balance their turns by the breeze on their faces. Cold air on the cheek to the inside of the turn meant the aeroplane was slipping; a draught on the outside cheek was evidence of a skid. Breeze-free and the turn was balanced. For many years, even well beyond the First World War, this reliance upon wind-on-cheek convinced some pilots and designers that it would be impossible to fly an aircraft with a fully-enclosed cockpit.

The ponderous ailerons limited an Avro's aerobatic prowess in the rolling plane to a rudder-inspired half-roll or a barrel roll, but the machine's low wing loading made loops tight and easily accomplished from a dive to 90 mph (cruise speed was 65-70 mph), and the Avro would spin enthusiastically (and without being asked to if stalled carelessly), though it spun slowly and lost so little altitude with each rotation that it was an ideal mount for performing the attractive but now rarely seen falling leaf manoeuvre in which the aeroplane descends in a series of checked spins in alternate directions.

On landing the Avro's rubber bungee cord suspension would magnify every bounce into a kangaroo ride across the airfield if a student misjudged his touchdown, with the lack of a conventional throttle denying him a smooth application of power to recover. On touch-and-go landings it was vital to remember to lean the mixture set-

Right: A Sunbeam-engined Avro, restored to represent the first aircraft operated by the Australian airline Quantas.

Below: This Avro 504K is part of Canada's National Aeronautical Collection.

ting once the engine was running smoothly again after take-off, for the Mono was very prone to cutting out if the mixture was too rich, and the lightly-loaded high-drag Avro would quickly lose flying speed and stall within seconds unless its nose was pushed down swiftly to maintain flying speed. The correct technique in the event of a rich cut (which resulted in the Mono trailing a plume of black smoke to alert everyone on the ground to the pilot's predicament) was to pull back the petrol lever and wait seven or eight seconds for the engine to pick up again on the leaned petrol/air mixture. An anxious student would often fail to wait long enough, push the petrol lever back up, further enriching the mixture and ensuring a forced landing, then shut off the fuel again just before touchdown, whereupon the engine would unchoke itself and come back on again. Having

seemingly solved the problem the unfortunate trainee would climb away in relief, forgetting to return the petrol lever, and would have his Mono cut dead through fuel starvation.

For all that, students and instructors alike developed a strong affection for the Avro, reflected in this song composed to the tune of 'That Old Fashioned Mother of Mine' and sung around Royal Air Force Flying Schools for two decades:

Just an old-fashioned Avro with old-fashioned
   ways,
And a kick that says back-fire to you,
An old Mono engine that konks out and stays
When toil of a long flight is through.
Though the pressure will drop and it loses its
   prop
And the pilot's inclined to resign,
I'll rejoice till I die that I learnt how to fly
On that old-fashioned Avro of mine!
There are finer machines with much better
   windscreens,
And whose pilots don't know what a dud engine
   means,
But my good old Avro can loop, roll or spin,
And there isn't a field that I can't put her in,
That old-fashioned Avro of mine.

Indeed there can have been few English fields into which pilots did *not* put an Avro, for surplus 504s became the workhorses of post-war barnstormers and touring airshows. They were cheap (some sold for as little as £25), plentiful and could be easily modified to carry two or even three passengers in the open rear cockpit. Thus many demobbed Royal Flying Corps pilots plied their trade from farmers' fields, beaches and fairgrounds at 'five bob a flip'. In 1919 ten thousand passengers flew from Blackpool in a two-month period, while Captain Percival Phillips, a buccaneering Cornishman, estimated that he personally flew 91,250 passengers in his fleet of bright red Avros in the 1920s and 1930s. Sir Alan Cobham, the great pioneer aviator and champion of aviation, also used Avros for joy-riding and in his touring airshow acts, which included a wing-walking performance by a member of his team named Martin Hearn, who would take an identically-dressed dummy aloft with him and fling it from the aeroplane while he hid in the cockpit. Hearn's act was abandoned after an Irish tour where the crowds included an unusually high percentage of pregnant women who fainted when the 'wingwalker' seemingly fell to his death.

The Avro: a gentle, forgiving aeroplane, which rewarded those who respected it and seldom 'bit' those who abused it.

With engine hours strictly limited ground-manoeuvring of the Shuttleworth Avro is left to manpower.

BECHEREAU'S BEAUTIES

Great aircraft are often the children of fortunate marriages, the result of the mating of like minds. Such was the case with the SPAD scouts, which combined the talents of two great engineers in aeroplanes commonly regarded as the best fighters of the First World War. SPAD was an acronym for the *Société Pour l'Aviation et ses*

Dérivées, which the cross-channel pioneer Louis Blériot founded in 1914 when he took over the rival *Société Pour les Appareils Dépérdussin*. Blériot contrived the new company title to retain the SPAD abbreviation with which silk manufacturer Armand Dépérdussin had gained a reputation for inventiveness, innovation and performance dating back to the 1912 Gordon Bennett Cup air race and the 1913 Coupe Jacques Schneider.

Among the assets which Blériot acquired from the near-bankrupted Dépérdussin was his tech-

nical director, one Louis Béchéreau, who had designed the monocoque Dépérdussin racers with which France took the world air speed record at 200 kilometres per hour and won – for the only time in its history – Jacques Schneider's seaplane race. Béchéreau's first designs under Blériot's direction were spectacularly unpromising, but late in 1915 he began work on a new single-seat fighter with one eye cast enviously at the powerful, efficient water-cooled aero engines which his German adversaries were using.

Rotary engines, then dominant as aircraft powerplants, offered power enough, but the more power you drew from them the greater the gyroscopic forces imposed on the aeroplane by the spinning motor and the worse the handling problems facing the unfortunate pilot. By happy chance a young Swiss engineer named Marc Birkigt, co-founder and chief designer of the Hispano-Suiza motor car company, was at the time developing an aluminium block water-cooled V-8 engine which had 500 fewer parts than the German Mercedes aero engine and offered an excellent power-to-weight ratio.

An 'arranged marriage' between Birkigt's fine powerplant and Béchéreau's airframe brought forth the first SPAD scout. Béchéreau eschewed the expensive, labour-intensive tulip wood mono-

coque construction which he had employed on his pre-war racers in favour of a more conventional but tremendously strong airframe. The first aeroplane, designated SPAD S.VII and powered by one of Birkigt's 140 hp Hispano-Suizas, made its maiden flight from the *Aviation Militaire* airfield at Villacoublay, south of Paris in April 1916. It was a bluff-looking compact biplane with dihedral-less unstaggered wings of very thin section, the ribs set close together for strength, while the intersections of flying and landing wires were supported by wooden braces, giving it the appearance of a two-bay biplane.

Despite its greater weight the new SPAD was clearly a better performer than the lightly-built Nieuport 17 which was then the *Aviation Militaire*'s principal scout, except in manoeuvrability. The SPAD, with a maximum speed of 122 mph, was faster, and it could outclimb the Nieuport, but it could not match the lighter machine's agility. Unfortunately the Nieuports were prone to structural failure, particularly during high speed dives when upper wing fabric and often the wings themselves would depart from the rest of the airframe. Béchéreau's dreadnought structure was so dense that it could be relied upon to hold together even after combat damage, and while it might not match the Nieuport's

sprightly handling, it provided a steady platform for its single synchronised Vickers 0.303 machine-gun.

Among the first *escadrilles de chasse* to receive the new SPADs when they arrived on the Western Front in September 1916 was *Groupe de Combat 12*, an elite and formidable band of pilots who called themselves *Les Cicognes* – The Storks. *Les Cicognes'* association with the SPAD was later to persuade Marc Birkigt to adopt their stylised stork insignia as a radiator emblem on his post-war Hispano-Suiza cars where its effectiveness at impaling unfortunate pedestrians was said to have been second only to the SPAD's combat record! Prominent among *Les Cicognes* was Lieutenant Georges Guynemer, who was among the first pilots to receive a SPAD S.VII and lost no time in demonstrating its superiority by downing three German aircraft in five minutes on 23 September 1916.

Such was the demand for Béchéreau's new machine that by 1917 SPADs were being built faster than any other aeroplanes in the world, at eight factories in France and two in Britain. The air arms of Belgium, Britain, Italy, Russia and the United States had placed orders for S.VIIs, of which 5,600 were eventually manufactured in France, with others built under licence abroad.

But the pace of aircraft development speeded up as the war progressed, and as 1917 dawned so the German Albatros D.V and Anthony Fokker's Dr.I triplane eroded some of the S.VII's combat superiority. Birkigt had further developed his splendid engine, extracting 150, 180 and 200 hp from it and Louis Béchéreau took advantage of the increased power available to him to further improve his design with the SPAD S.XII, a cannon-armed machine suggested to him by Georges Guynemer. Between the banks of the Hispano-Suiza's cylinders they mounted a 37 mm

Hotchkiss cannon which fired through a hollow crankshaft and propeller hub which were raised in line with the gun by a geared drive. It was called *moteur cannon*, and with it Guynemer shot down four enemy aircraft while his *Les Cicognes* colleague René Fonck, the highest 'scoring' French pilot of the war and 'Allied Ace of Aces', claimed 11 of his 75 confirmed kills with the cannon, but the S.XII was not a success. The Hotchkiss had no positive means of aiming, the only possible technique being to fire a trial burst with the SPAD's Vickers gun, which also served to forewarn the selected target. And since the cannon was a hand-loaded single shot weapon a poorly aimed shot gave an enemy plenty of time to take evasive action. That, a recoil which all but stopped the aeroplane short in the air, and cordite fumes from the cannon threatening to choke its pilot, brought the SPAD S.XII's career to a swift end.

Meanwhile Béchéreau was working on his next and finest SPAD development, which combined a 200 hp (later 220 and 235 hp) Hispano-Suiza with two Vickers guns to give the SPAD S.XIII a 30 mph speed advantage over contemporary German scouts with equivalent firepower. The first S.XIII, which was an entirely new aeroplane rather than a developed S.VII, flew on 4 April 1917 and immediately went into production as a replacement for earlier SPADs and Nieuport 28s. Veteran combat pilots from both sides in the First World War rated the SPAD S.VII and S.XIII as the best fighters of the war. They were also the most numerous, for some 14,400 were built, a fighter aircraft production total not exceeded until the Second World War. If orders from the United States had not been cancelled after the Armistice the total would have risen to more than 25,000.

SPADs were pilot's aeroplanes, demanding in their handling, but rewarding and responsive to the skilled touch. The thin airfoil chosen by Béchéreau and the excess of power provided by Birkigt's engines gave the aeroplanes an edge over adversaries in rate of climb, but the lack of dihedral made SPADs laterally sensitive. They were not 'hands off' machines at any time, least of all on landing when a high sink rate could develop power off. A SPAD had to be 'motored in'. But, like Birkigt's automobiles, they were machines for the connoisseur, eminently satisfying, totally trustworthy. And the pilots loved them. Captain Eddie Rickenbacker, the leading United States air ace of the First World War who flew with the 94th Aero (Uncle Sam's Hat in Ring) Squadron in France and scored 26 victories said of the S.XIII: 'It was more impressive than any other airplane, any other automobile, any other piece of equipment I had ever seen, the ultimate aircraft in the war.'

Left, far left and previous page: Replica SPAD S.VII with modern four cylinder horizontally-opposed engine skilfully disguised under a mock Hispano-Suiza cowling.

SPADs were indeed fine fighting machines. They had speed, firepower and great strength. SPAD pilots had no fears of structural failure when diving steeply to pursue or escape pursuit, as they had with the Nieuports. Béchéreau's stalwart airframe would hold together under the most unreasonable stresses, and the SPAD's stability, which denied it the manoeuvrability of some contemporaries, made it a superlative gun platform. Its faults were few: the coolant header tank for the Hispano-Suiza engine was mounted in the upper wing centre section, perfectly positioned to scald the pilot if it sprang a leak or was punctured by gunfire; and the SPAD was difficult to land because of the high sink rate and the low pilot's position – akin to sitting on a toboggan – which obscured forward vision.

It was exactly the kind of machine which a talented and determined pilot might exploit to great advantage. George Guynemer, an intense 21-year-old who lived by the dictum 'if one has not given everything one has given nothing', destroyed 54 German aircraft, mostly on SPADs. He fought for two years without rest, drove himself to the edge of mental and physical fatigue and finally disappeared in his SPAD S.XIII on 11 September 1917 over Poelcapelle, apparently the victim of an attack by a flight of Albatros D.Vs. René Fonck of *Les Cicognes*, a fine marksman and master of the deflection shot with the twin Vickers of his S.XIII, four times brought down two enemy aircraft in a day, and once accounted for six, three of them in such short order that the wrecks all fell within a quarter of a square mile. *Les Cicognes'* SPADs destroyed 200 enemy aircraft in their first six months of combat, playing an instrumental role in gaining supremacy in the air over the Western Front. Truly the SPAD was a hunter's weapon, honed to a fine edge by the talents of two remarkable engineers.

for the obsolete Be2cs and 2es. The British & Colonial Aeroplane Company refused an offer to licence build the R.E.8 and instead had chief designer Frank Barnwell create a new lightweight two seater known as the Bristol R.2A, powered by a 120 hp Beardmore engine. A further variant, the R.2B, was planned with a 150 hp Hispano-Suiza, but both were abandoned by Barnwell when the 190 hp Rolls-Royce Falcon became available. Here was an ideal *fighter*

THE BIFF

In 1918 a British aviation magazine published an anonymous poem which ran:

Many a first rate joy ride
Have I had on 'em last and first.
And many a strut have I had go phut,
And many a wheel tyre burst.
But none of them know the secret
Of making my heart rejoice
Like a well-rigged Bristol Fighter
With a two-six-four Rolls-Royce.

Yet there was little about the Bristol Fighter's service debut to make the heart rejoice. The first Brisfits (or Biffs) to join the air offensive along the British Front in April 1917 were decimated by their German opponents.

The design originated not as a fighter but as a reconnaissance aircraft, competing with the Royal Aircraft Factory's R.E.8 as a replacement

The Shuttleworth Trust's prized airworthy Bristol Fighter.

powerplant. Barnwell set about re-designing his machines, and the prototype F.2A was ready to fly on 9 September 1916, with a Hispano-engined variant following six weeks later. A significant feature of the design was the way in which Barnwell mounted the aircraft's fuselage midway between the mainplanes, bringing the upper wing level with the pilot's eyes (and thus providing him with a view over its top surface). Armament on this first British two-seat fighter consisted of a forward-firing Vickers gun mounted beneath the engine cowling and a Lewis gun on a Scarff ring mounting at the observer's station.

Two squadrons of F.2As were readied for the spring offensive of 1917, and six aircraft of 48 Squadron made their first patrol on 5 April, led by Captain W. Leefe Robinson, V.C. Only two returned to the squadron's base at Bellevue. The rest fell victim to Albatros D.IIIs of *Jagdstaffel 11*

led by Manfred von Richthofen in a brief combat near Douai. The cause of this debacle had little to do with the Bristol, for the fault lay in the way in which the aeroplanes had been used. Their pilots, accustomed to conventional two-seater tactics, used their armament purely defensively and, perhaps believing totally unfounded rumours that the Bristol had structural weaknesses, failed to take advantage of the machine's speed and manoeuvrability, which enabled it to be fought exactly like a smaller scout. The lesson was quickly learned, and once crews grew accustomed to using the Bristol offensively, and keeping the observer's Lewis gun for tail protection, the aircraft became a formidable weapon. By the end of April 1917 48 Squadron's F.2As were returning from patrols well behind German lines without loss.

Official confidence, on the wain after the first Douai fiasco, was quickly restored and Barnwell further improved upon his design with better pilot visibility, greater fuel and ammunition storage and new tail surfaces. In its definitive F.2B form the Brisfit was powered by no fewer than 17 different types of engine, of which the most common (and best loved) was the super-

lative 275 hp Rolls-Royce Falcon III, a water-cooled V-12 powerplant which was a joy to handle compared to the recalcitrant, idiosynchratic rotaries.

Alongside the single seat scouts such as the Sopwith Pup and Camel the Brisfit was a mammoth, with a wingspan of 39 feet 3 inches and a loaded weight of close to 3,000 pounds. The cockpit was compact, with pilot and observer placed back to back almost level with the lower wing's trailing edge so that both enjoyed an excellent field of view in all directions save for immediately below and behind, whence came most of the attacks resulting in early Brisfit losses.

On the F.2B provision was made for mounting two Lewis guns on the Scarff ring in addition to the Vickers mounted between the two banks of the Falcon's cylinders. With three guns the Brisfit was a radical departure from all previous tactical thinking, and was the subject of much

controversy as to whether the pilot should place the aeroplane in a position which would give his *observer* a good firing line or whether *he* should engage with the front gun and leave the observer to beat off attackers from the rear. The big aeroplane's fine handling characteristics, excellent manoeuvrability and great strength finally determined the latter tactic, and to great effect. Within six months of its introduction with 11 Squadron the F.2B Brisfit had convincingly demonstrated its superiority (one 11 Squadron pilot, Lieutenant A. E. McKeever, destroyed 30 enemy aircraft in this period), and in the early months of 1918 Brisfit crews found that German pilots were reluctant to engage in combat with more than two Bristols.

Although the Brisfit was manoeuvrable few would disagree that it was heavy on the controls. The elevators reportedly were made especially heavy because the original specification called

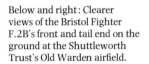
Below and right: Clearer views of the Bristol Fighter F.2B's front and tail end on the ground at the Shuttleworth Trust's Old Warden airfield.

for the aircraft to have a maximum diving speed of 400 mph which, though highly improbable even in a vertical terminal velocity dive, would easily have resulted in structural failure with light control forces. The ailerons too were sluggish and it was said, with some validity, that you could recognise a Brisfit pilot by the well-developed state of his biceps!

The aeroplane's overall performance was excellent. With the Falcon III engine a Brisfit's top speed in level flight was 125 mph, its rate of climb in excess of 800 feet per minute and its service ceiling around 18,000 feet. One former Brisfit pilot recalled: 'The pilot could enter a dog-fight and turn almost as quickly and on almost as small a radius as the best single seater. He could fling his machine about, go into vertical dives, pull it out quickly, turn it on its back, spin it, roll it and generally do every sort of manoeuvre if the need arose. And all the time there was the comfortable feeling that the observer was there with his pair of Lewis guns, watching and protecting.' Casualties among Brisfit observers was very high, and their heroism contributed much to the aeroplane's reputation. Acts of prodigious courage occurred in defending the aeroplane from the exposed observer's station with no engine or surrounding structure to protect the gunner. Yet there was never a shortage of volunteers for Bristol Fighters.

Typical of those who flew the Brisfit was Captain F. West of 8 Squadron, who won the Victoria Cross for his part in the bombing of the Somme bridges on 10 August 1918 in support of armoured ground forces. The incident was reported in the *London Gazette*:

'Captain West, flying with Lieutenant J. A. G. Haslam as observer, noticed much enemy activity about Roye, then the objective of the tank attack. He dropped his bombs with effect, but when about to return was attacked by six enemy aeroplanes. Early in the engagement one of his legs was partially severed by an explosive bullet and he fell powerless into the controls, rendering the machine for the time unmanageable. Lifting his disabled leg he regained control of the machine, and although wounded in the other leg, he, with surpassing bravery and devotion to duty, manoeuvred his machine so skilfully that his observer was enabled to get several bursts into the enemy machines, which drove them away. Captain West then, with rare courage and determination, desperately wounded as he was, brought his machine over our lines and landed safely. Exhausted by his exertions he fainted, but on regaining consciousness insisted on writing his report.'

By the end of the Great War Brisfits equipped fourteen full squadrons, and the aeroplane was

destined to become a mainstay of the embryo Royal Air Force in peacetime, remaining in production (it was built in ten factories in Britain and three in the United States) until 1926, and in Royal Air Force service until 1932, performing capably in many roles for which Frank Barnwell had not designed it. 4,469 were built. In recognition of the Brisfit's wartime achievements the British Government awarded the British & Colonial Aeroplane Company £80,000.

It was a generous gesture, but not entirely a fitting tribute to a fine aeroplane. For that let us turn again to that unnamed poet and his 'Ballad of the Bristol Fighter':

She leans at her place on the tarmac
Like a tiger crouched for a spring,
From the arching spine of her fuselage line
To the ample spread of her wing.
With her tyres like sinews taughtened
And her tail-skid's jaunty twist,
Her grey-cowled snout juts grimly out
Like a tight-clenched boxer's fist.

Is there a sweeter music,
A more contenting sound,
Than the purring clop of her broad-curved prop
As it gently ticks around?
Open her out to crescendo
To a deep-toned swelling roar,
Till she quivers and rocks as she strains at the
  chocks
And clamours again to soar.

Whisk 'em away, my hearties,
Taxi her into wind,
Then away we skim on a spinning rim
With the tail well up behind.
Hold her down to a hundred,
Then up in a climbing turn
And off we sweep in a speckless sky
Till we catch our breath in the air Alp-high.
I wouldn't exchange my seat, not I,
For a thousand pounds to burn.

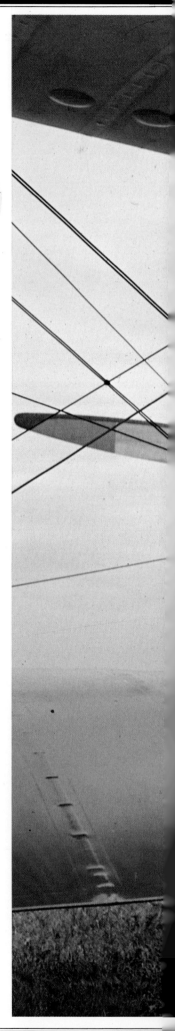

JENNY WAS NO LADY

You would hear the sound of the OX-5 engine coming way across the fields, and you would be out of the house in an instant, hands shielding your eyes against the sunlight, scanning the summer sky for . . . Yes! There it was, and it was heading right your way. An *airplane!*

You had seen them before, once or twice, but this one was much lower. You could make out the cat's cradle of bracing wires between its long yellow wings, and the dark figure of the pilot. He was almost above you now, tipping the airplane up on a wing. You waved frantically. And he waved back, so low that you could see his helmeted face grinning at you. For a moment you scarcely dared hope that he might be landing, then the OX-5 went quiet and you caught the swish of wind through wires and you started running. . . .

You arrived, breathless, at the fence, and there in the pasture was the most beautiful sight you had ever beheld. A real airplane, and beside it the aviator in his leather coat and whipcord breeches, wiping a smear of oil from his wind-tanned face. You scarcely dared speak, but managed to blurt out: 'You in trouble mister?' 'Nope, plannin' on stayin' here a few days givin' rides, is all.' 'Giving *airplane* rides?' 'Yup. Five bucks for five minutes. Greatest experience of your life.' Your crestfallen face told him that you did not *have* five dollars. 'Tell you what. You help me fix my sign on that fence over there, fetch some gas from town for my airplane and help me load her up with passengers and I'll show you and

your folks your home from the air tomorrow.' You stopped just long enough to point out that you had heard your mother say once that you would never get *her* up in an airplane and could you have two rides instead, before you grabbed the canvas sign which read *Airplane Rides – $5* and started running again, pausing mid-step with one final question: 'Mister, what kind of airplane is that?' He told you it was a Jenny, and you figured that must be his wife's, or maybe his girl's name. It didn't sound right for an airplane.

Jenny. Not short for Jennifer, but long for JN-4, the Curtiss Military Tractor Biplane ordered late in 1914 for the US Army to replace the Curtiss and Wright pusher biplanes which had suffered appalling fatality rates in training military pilots. Paradoxically this machine, which was the first commercially successful mass-production American aeroplane, and one which was destined to bring flying within reach of hundreds of thousands, perhaps millions of people across the United States, was designed by an Englishman, one B. Douglas Thomas. Thomas had worked for the Avro and Sopwith companies in Britain. Glenn Curtiss enticed him to Hammondsport to design a tractor biplane for the Army, and this aircraft, the Curtiss J, combined with the best features of the Curtiss N, resulted in the JN, whose designation prompted an obvious phonetic corruption to 'Jenny'.

The massive expansion of US pilot training which followed America's belated entry into the First World War brought huge orders for Jennies, met by the Curtiss company and six sub-contractors in the United States and by

Above and right: A beautifully restored Curtiss JN-4D owned by retired airline captain Dan Neumann in the United States.

Canadian Aeroplanes Limited in Canada, whose 'Jennies' were called Canucks. By the time peace returned 6,070 Jennies had been delivered, and one in every ten Canadian and American pilots had trained on them. The US Army then had a huge surplus of new and nearly-new aeroplanes which they did not want. Curtiss bought back 2,000 Jennies, paying barely 10 per cent of what the Army had paid him to manufacture them, and the aircraft were refurbished where necessary and marketed commercially as 'a bargain every aeronautical buyer must consider'.

In truth the first surplus Jennies were not that much of a bargain, priced at $4,000. But within a few years surplus Canucks being dumped as British war surplus were down to $1,500, and eventually prices fell to absurdly low levels, some changing hands for as little as $50 by the late 1920s. This wholesale dumping is cited by some people for preventing the development of new and better aircraft in the post-war years. Perhaps so, but the Jenny's bargain basement price tag did spark off that romantic and short-lived era, the age of the barnstormer. Barnstormers were drifters, gipsy pilots turned loose from the Army with no trade save for aviating and no hope of employment. Six hundred dollars could buy a Jenny or a Canuck, and the crates they came in doubled as shanty homes when times were hard, which they often were, especially in the later years when flying was no longer a novelty and $5 for five minutes was the best you could hope for, with a few aerobatics thrown in if the passengers could stand it.

The Jennies grew tired, but they were undemanding. A strand or two of a farmer's bailing wire, a patch of cotton canvas and the attention of any blacksmith would cure most of their ills. The leaky old OX-5 engine, which Curtiss's advertising assured was 'one of the most reliable' was anything but, and was certain to let you down (in both senses) at least once a day, but a good morning's work would buy a new one and propellers could be bought for $5, so the occasional crack-up was not too much of a problem. When the novelty of aeroplane rides began to pale, the more inventive (or reckless) fliers took to selling their skills

Above: Dan Neumann waiting to take-off in his Jenny at the Experimental Aircraft Association convention at Oshkosh, Wisconsin.

Left: US Army Curtiss Jennies on a training flight.

Below and left: More views of Dan Neumann's Jenny, restored in the colours of the US Army 27th Aero Squadron.

to Hollywood, and the old Jenny became a movie star. She was perfect for aerial stunts: her wings were long and held together with a forest of struts, king-posts, wingtip bows and bracing wires to provide plenty of handholds for a man strolling about them in flight, and the plain axle between the wheels made a perfect aerial trapeze.

Unlikely tales abound about the Hollywood stunt fliers. There was Daredevil Al Wilson, who taught Cecil B. De Mille to fly. His tricks included flying a Jenny off the roof of a building in the Los Angeles business district, having first dismantled it to get it up there, and changing the wheel on a Jenny while standing on the wing of another one flying just below it. Gladys Ingle, the

Left and Right: Earl Daugherty at work below and on top of a Jenny for movie cameras. Daugherty was one of the first barnstormers and aerial stuntment, working with wing walker Wes May in California in the early 1920s. Below: the great Ormer Locklear, 'the man who walked on wings', trapeze-hanging from a Jenny's undercarriage spreader bar.

only woman member of a group of stunt fliers called the 13 Black Cats used to give aerial archery demonstrations on top of a Jenny's wing in flight, shooting arrows at a target set up on one wingtip while she stood on the other. She made more than 300 plane-to-plane transfers in flight. Other members of the 13 Black Cats staged bar-room card games and brawls on a Jenny's wing!

Far right: A cat's cradle of bracing wires made the Jenny a natural mount for stuntmen and wing walkers. Right: Faultless restoration of a Jenny's cockpit by American airline captain Dan Neumann. Below: The prototype Curtiss JN-4D photographed in 1917.

A legendary figure among the stunt fliers was Ormer Locklear, who had served as an instructor with the US Army Air Corps at Barron Field, Texas. Heroic tales about Locklear are legion, and probably quite true. The most popular alleges that he was flying a Jenny on a Signals Corps mission one day in 1917 when the trailing radio antenna he had thrown out snagged the aircraft's tail bracing wires. Locklear is supposed to have climbed from his cockpit and squirmed his way back to the Jenny's tail to untangle the aerial, just in time to receive a cryptic signal from his commanding officer: *Locklear, UR grounded.* Another feat came when he was instructing a student and saw the radiator cap blow off his Jenny's OX-5. This time Locklear is said to have left his student to keep the Jenny flying level while he climbed up over the centre-section, stuffed a rag in the radiator filler, and, as an encore, climbed down and sat on the axle. On another occasion he walked the length of a Jenny's wing in flight to demonstrate the aeroplane's stability to a doubting pupil.

Whatever the truth of his Army exploits, Locklear was among the earliest of the movie stunt fliers, flying for the film *The Great Air Robbery* in 1919. His task was to make a plane-to-plane change then drop from the Jenny onto a moving train. The following year he became the first person to be charged with 'disturbing the peace in the air' when he looped over a Los Angeles park, and was rewarded with a contract from Universal Studios. He celebrated by making a plane-to-plane change over the sports stadium in which Jack Dempsey and Jess Willard were contesting

the world boxing title. Locklear was not only celebrated among the stunt fliers for his daring; he was also noted for performing all his antics wearing a smart tweed business suit. He died on 2 August 1920 while filming the MGM movie *The Skywayman*. Locklear was flying a Jenny at night and was supposed to spin down around a parachute flare, illuminated by wingtip lights and powerful searchlights on the ground. What happened will never be known for sure, but the Jenny crashed into an oil well sludge pool and exploded, burning Locklear and his passenger. Perhaps he was disorientated by the lights; possibly he lost control of the aeroplane trying to avoid the burning flare which threatened to set fire to his machine.

There was no shortage of replacements, men like 'Smiles' O'Timmons, a one-legged, one-armed stuntman whose artificial leg once punctured the fabric of a Jenny during a wing walk, trapping him among the broken ribs. O'Timmons calmly unstrapped the leg and hopped back into the cockpit, to the horror of a watching crowd who could see the leg still sticking up through the wing! Another stuntman named Wes May actually rode a bicycle along a Jenny's wing in flight. A cameraman filming the event was so captivated that he kept cranking his camera even after the aircraft's propeller had sliced off one of his fingers. And a mechanic with Ivan Gates Flying Circus, one of the biggest touring airshows in the United States, encapsulated those hard times with a cable to his boss, who had cautioned him about wasting money on Western Union. It happened that his pilot, Swede Meyerhoffer, had been killed swinging his Jenny's propeller. His telegram was succinct and very much to the point: *Swede cranked prop. Prop killed Swede. Send new prop.*

Jenny was no lady. She was awkward and ugly. She was moody and temperamental, tattered, torn and down-at-heel. She sagged and she sighed. But she was the sweetheart of a generation and the founder of an industry. I can find no better tribute to her than this one from an Army pilot:

Old Jane, we rode the air together
In perfect and in bumpy weather;
We slipped and skidded through the sky
Those first few weeks I tried to fly;
None as kind as you, none crude as I –
Old Jane.

First loves we were. No other ships
Can ever put you in eclipse;
New buses that I navigate
Coy, flighty, preening, bold, sedate,
Lack things I want, have tricks I hate –
Make me but more appreciate
Old Jane.

IMPERIAL ELEGANCE

Passengers called them 'Flying Bananas'. Pilots from rival companies, feeling smug in their sleek new Douglases and Lockheeds, made unkind remarks about aeroplanes with their own built-in headwinds. Yet, for all the ribaldry, Imperial Airways' slow and steady aerial galleons, their Handley Page H.P.42 biplane airliners, won envied reputations for safety, dependability and passenger comfort seldom matched by an other aeroplane in the history of commercial air transport.

The H.P.42 dates back to the spring of 1928 when Imperial Airways, the British civil avia-

tion flag carrier of the between-wars period, invited tenders for the supply of a fleet of new aeroplanes for the Empire airmail route to India, stipulating that the aircraft should offer 'the greatest safety, highest possible paying load capacity and lowest cost of operation' and have a stalling speed not exceeding 52 mph. Beyond that, tendering manufacturers were to be allowed 'the greatest possible freedom of expression for their own ideas.' Handley Page Ltd's tenders for four Eastern route and four Western route (European services) aircraft were accepted and in July 1929 a furnished wooden fuselage mock-up of the aircraft was displayed at the Aero Exhibition at Olympia, where its Pullman-style interior complete with cocktail bar drew much approval.

The H.P.42 was a four-engined design with the

uncowled radial engines arranged 'two-up, two-down'. The prototype, named *Hannibal*, made its first flight from the Handley Page factory airfield at Radlett, Hertfordshire on 14 November 1930 after several days of hopping along the field, and three days later was demonstrated to Press and public, getting off the ground with a run of just sixty yards and giving an impressive demonstration with three of its four engines throttled back. Despite its apparent outdatedness, with heavy Warren Girder strut bracing and triple-finned biplane tail unit, the H.P.42 made up for its lack of external beauty with elegant comforts within. The slight 'kink' in the fuselage (hence the 'banana' nickname) brought the passenger door close to the ground, so that flights of steps were not necessary for boarding, and once they stepped into its cabin passengers found inlaid wood

Left: *Hannibal,* one of the Eastern H.P. 42s, pictured at Karachi.

Above left: *Helena* cruising on top of cloud cover for an Imperial Airways publicity picture.

Right: Unloading baggage from an H.P.42

Below: The low ground clearance afforded by the H.P. 42's 'banana' fuselage is evident in this shot of passengers boarding *Heracles* at Croydon.

panelling, comfortable armchairs, long picture windows, two lavatories, duplicate instruments and individual controls for heating and ventilation at each seat. The galley, toilets and baggage compartment were located between the two passenger saloons in an area adjacent to the four engines, thus further reducing noise levels in the soundproofed cabins, while the thoughtful use of anhedralled centre sections to the lower wings enabled the wing/fuselage junctions to be placed above the passenger saloon ceiling so that travellers might enjoy an uninterrupted view of the landscape.

The H.P.42E 'Eastern' variants for service on the India and South Africa Empire routes were powered by four 550 hp Bristol Jupiter XI.F nine-cylinder engines. The H.P.42W 'Western' aircraft for the London-Paris cross-channel shuttle and other continental services had Jupiter X.FBMs. The 'Es', adopting the names *Hannibal*, *Horsa* (originally *Hecate*, which was thought to have unfortunate connotations), *Hanno* and *Hadrian*, carried 12 passengers in each forward and rear saloon; the 'Ws', also reflecting Imperial Airways' new policy of adopting names from history and mythology, were called *Heracles*, *Horatius*, *Helena* and *Hengist* (the latter instead of *Hesperides*, which Imperial staff found too difficult to spell), and carried 20 and 18 passengers respectively in fore and aft cabins, with reduced baggage space. The operational crew comprised a captain, first officer, radio officer and one or two stewards.

On 11 June 1931 it fell to one of the Eastern

aircraft, *Hannibal*, to inaugurate the London-Paris Silver Wing service from Croydon Airport to Le Bourget before journeying to its base at Cairo in August. By early in 1932 all eight H.P.42s were in service with Imperial Airways, and the Western aircraft were a familiar sight at Croydon, where their short take-off and landing characteristics enabled them to operate directly off the concrete Customs apron rather than from the grass airfield proper in a moderate wind. While the 600-foot take-off run and 65 mph landing speed of the H.P.42 could be an asset, it was also the aircraft's Achilles' heel. A brisk headwind eating into its leisurely 95 mph cruise speed could prove embarrassing. One former Imperial Airways' captain recalls taking more than an hour to cross the narrowest stretch of the English Channel.

Nonetheless, for a return fare of £6. 15s. 0d. Imperial's Silver Wing service proved immensely popular with businessmen. Passengers departed from the Airways Terminus at Victoria Station at 8.15 am or 11.45 am and arrived at the Hotel Bohy-Lafayette on Rue Lafayette in the heart of Paris 3 hours and 45 minutes later. *En route* they were served breakfast or lunch (and an excellent lunch it was, with fresh vegetables and fine wines). *Speed Without Hurry* was the Imperial motto. Their boast that 'a complete service of meals – breakfast, lunch and tea – is served on the flight between London and Paris' was unfortunately worded, however, and drew from C. G. Grey, waspish editor of *The Aeroplane*, the wry comment that he 'had no idea that the distance was so great, or alternatively that Imperial

Airways' big four-engined airliners took so long to get there.'

Smoking on board was strictly prohibited, as one passenger found to his cost when he was fined £10 by a Croydon court for lighting up an after dinner cigar aboard *Heracles*. Smoking aside, Imperial Airways' customers were *always* right. A senior H.P.42 captain was summarily dismissed for being (perhaps justifiably) rude to an especially tiresome passenger. Captains were supposed to be models of diplomacy, but many of the early Imperial pilots were what was euphemistically referred to as 'rough diamonds', former Royal Flying Corps NCO pilots whose turn of phrase did not always fit the public's image of an airline captain. An apocryphal story has it that genteel passengers aboard a Silver Wing flight to Paris overheard an H.P.42 captain make several requests for his radio officer to haul in the ensign which was flown from the cockpit roof before take-off and after landing as they taxied out at Croydon. No response was forthcoming, whereupon the captain was heard to bellow the non-standard instruction: *Mister, pull that bloody rag in!*

The Eastern H.P.42s flew out of Cairo to Karachi and Delhi. The journey from England to India took six and a half days, stopping at night *en route*. Officers of the Raj were urged 'to gain precious weeks leave' by travelling with Imperial Airways, and 'English foods or Fresh Indian fruits can be exchanged between friends as never before'. On these long-haul routes a close rapport grew up between passengers and crew. It was not uncommon for a captain to dine with his charges

Contemporary advertisements for Eastern and Western H.P.42 services.

on night stops, nor was he above asking them to help refuel the aeroplane on those occasions when a landing at one of Imperial's unattended desert fuel stores became necessary before continuing their journey. In Europe the H.P.42s eventually ranged beyond Paris to Brussels, Basle, Cologne and Zurich, and were in great demand at home for day trips to events such as the Grand National horse race and for joy-riding, including 'tea flights' over central London.

Utilisation was high. *Heracles* flew 1,318,000 miles (at 95 mph remember) and carried 160,000 passengers in eight years' service, at a time when air travel was largely restricted to the middle and upper classes. Jointly *Hannibal, Horsa, Hanno, Hadrian, Heracles, Horatius, Helena* and *Hengist* flew more than 100,000 hours and 10 million miles without injury to a passenger, though not entirely without incident. *Hannibal* lost a propeller over Tonbridge just two months after inaugurating the Silver Wing service, but was successfully force-landed in a field. *Hengist*,

converted to Eastern standard, was destroyed in a hangar fire at Karachi in May 1937.

The seven remaining H.P.42s remained in service until the outbreak of the Second World War, when the aircraft were impressed into Royal Air Force service, some ferrying vital supplies – beer included – to troops in France. *Horatius* came to grief during an attempted landing on Tiverton golf course during a storm in November 1939; *Heracles, Hanno, Hadrian* and *Horsa* were all wrecked by gales on the ground; *Hannibal* disappeared in the Indian Ocean while being ferried back to England – the only fatal accident ever to befall an H.P.42; and *Helena* was eventually dismantled at Royal Naval Air Station Donibristle in 1941, her sumptuous forward cabin serving as a makeshift squadron office. Few relics of H.P.42s now remain – reminders of a genteel and gracious age. And, ironically, the total journey time between central London and Paris's boulevards has scarcely altered in 50 years.

Below: Corrugated skinning and 'two-up, two-down' engine configuration of the H.P.42 are well illustrated in this shot of *Heracles*.

WALTER'S WONDER PLANE

Mention the name Staggerwing at the Beech Aircraft Company's factory at Wichita, Kansas and you will probably be rewarded with a disapproving look. At Beech that classic American biplane is known as the Model 17 or, if you must, *The Beechcraft*, since at the time of its creation it was the only aeroplane which company founder Walter Beech had to offer. But go south to Tullahoma, Tennessee and you will find not only a museum bearing the Staggerwing name, but any number of people who will gladly tell you how their beloved 'Stag' came to earn its unofficial title.

It all began in 1924 when Walter Beech and his partners, Clyde Cessna and Lloyd Stearman, set up their own aircraft manufacturing company in Wichita. It was called the Travel Air Company, and they built sturdy, reliable biplanes and large single-engined monoplanes, one of which was placed first in the disastrous 1927 Dole Derby air race from San Francisco to Honolulu. By 1931 the partnership had dissolved. Cessna, convinced that the biplane's day was done, had set up his own company to build modern monoplanes, and Stearman had gone off to the West Coast, where he still continued to build biplanes.

Walter Beech had sold out Travel Air to the Curtiss-Wright company, but had stayed on to supervise development of the Mystery Ship racers which broke hundreds of long distance speed records in the late 1920s. But he was anxious to strike out on his own again, and in April 1932 he established the Beech Aircraft

Company in another part of Wichita, taking with him his chief designer Ted Wells, and the woman who had joined Travel Air as his secretary, became his wife and is to this day chief executive of the Beech Aircraft Company – Mrs. Olive Ann Beech. Beech and Wells were convinced they could build a biplane which would fly faster,

Above: Walter Beech.

Top: Man and Masterpiece. Walter Beech with 1934 Model B17L, the first Staggerwing to have a retractable undercarriage.

Above and centre right: The classic Travel Air biplane. The 'elephant ear' control surfaces gave it a superficial resemblance to the WWI Fokker D.7 fighter, and

Travel Airs were much used in movie-making, doubling for the German aircraft.

higher and further than their rivals' sleek new monoplanes. To say the least their plan was ambitious: the aeroplane would have a maximum speed of 200 mph, which was faster than contemporary US Army pursuit ships could go, but it would land at a sedate 60 mph.

The new Beechcraft Model 17 (Beech's last model for Travel Air had been the Model 16) was an exquisite four-seat cabin biplane powered by a tightly-cowled Wright Whirlwind radial engine of 420 hp, and it had an extraordinary back-staggered wing configuration with the upper wing set behind the lower – exactly the opposite of conventional biplane practice. It was not unique, having been used back in 1917 on the British Airco D.H.5 scout, but it was certainly unusual. The negative stagger layout offered both aerodynamic and engineering advantages, but Ted Wells claimed later that he chose it because he was supposed to test fly as well as engineer the new aeroplane, and he put the top wing back behind the windshield so that he would be able to see where he was going. It may be true, but the pilot on the Beechcraft's first flight on 4 November 1932 was Pete Hill, not Wells, and within a few days Hill had flown the

Top: The very first Staggerwing, the Model 17R pictured before delivery to the Ethyl Gasoline Corporation.

N1195V

tion at Miami, but buyers were not exactly beating on Beech's door. Indeed, though no-one at Beech will admit it now, those post-Depression days brought Walter and his new company perilously close to financial collapse, and he just kept solvent with prize money won by racing and demonstrating the prototype while building a second 17R ordered by an Oklahoma oil drilling company, whose pilot, Eddie Ross, was cheerfully given 100 days to live by his colleagues if he persisted in flying the aeroplane, which was no pussycat to handle. Ross proved the doubters wrong, though he allowed later that it was some while before he was really in total control of the Beechcraft.

With just one sale in two years Beech decided to attune his aircraft more closely to the market, substituting a 225 hp Jacobs engine for the Whirlwind and, to preserve some of the sparkling performance, arranging for the undercarriage to retract – then a rare feature on biplanes. This new Model B17L appeared in May 1934, shortly after Beech had begun advertising yet another variant, offered with an expensive Wright Cyclone engine, a massive brute of 690 hp which surely no one would want. But they did. Sanford Mills, a Maine-based textile company, placed an order for the $18,000, 250 mph A17F, which looked like a pugnacious bullfrog, would chase its own tail in a groundloop unless you opened the throttle very carefully, and was all but uncontrollable during the landing run. Two were built, the first machine eventually being sold to Howard Hughes as a trainer for his record-breaking H-1 racer, the second intended as an entry in the 1934 MacRobertson England-Australia air race, though it did not compete.

In all 781 Staggerwings were built, the most common being the D17S model with a 450 hp Pratt & Whitney Wasp Junior engine, which also powered the final, post-war G17S, perhaps the ultimate Staggerwing, hand-built in 1946 at a cost of $29,000. Today a pristine example would

aircraft at 201.2 mph – quite exceptional for a civilian light aeroplane at the time. To put the Beechcraft's achievement in modern day perspective, imagine a private aircraft which could outperform, say, an F-15 Eagle. In January 1933 the first Beech 17R was demonstrated in a number of speed dashes at the All-American Air Maneuvers in Miami, Florida, and it was during the course of one such run that an exhuberant airshow announcer exclaimed: 'Gee, look at that negative stagger wing Beechcraft go!' And thus the name Staggerwing was coined.

The Beechcraft attracted a great deal of atten-

Right: US Navy GB-2 Staggerwings awaiting delivery at the Beech factory at Wichita.

Left and left top: Back-staggered wing configuration and retractable undercarriage are evident in these views of D17S Staggerwings.

Above: A D17S Staggerwing restored in the colours of the first aircraft ordered by the US Army.

find ready buyers at $100,000. Why? Because the Staggerwing is held dearest in the hearts of American antique aeroplane buffs. The Tullahoma Staggerwing Museum is a shrine dedicated to an aeroplane which was ahead of its time, and to the people who flew it: Louise Thaden, whose friend Olive Ann Beech persuaded her husband that this young aviatrix should fly a Model 17 in the 1936 Bendix Continental Speed Dash between New York and Los Angeles, and was rewarded with victory at an average speed of 166 mph; Jimmy Haizlip, whose Beechcraft was brought to Europe aboard the airship *Hindenburg* and was subsequently flown by the great English pilot Owen Cathcart-Jones during the Spanish Civil War on high speed armaments purchasing flights throughout Europe; Captain Harold Farquhar, an ex-Coldstream Guardsman and First Secretary to the British Legation in Mexico, who flew a B17R around the world in 1935 and inspired the Beech sales catch phrase *The World Is Small When You Fly A Beechcraft*; and Prince Bernhardt of The Netherlands, who used a Staggerwing for his personal transportation in wartime exile.

There are some misguided people who will try to tell you that a Staggerwing is ugly. They are wrong. I would argue that it ranks high among the most beautiful of all biplanes, all sculptured curves and ellipses with barely a straight line to be seen, as if Walter Beech and Ted Wells had rough-hewn it from sandstone and left it to the

Top: 'Like a pugnacious bullfrog': the massive 690 hp Beech A17F.

Above: This 1934 Model B17L was powered by a 225 hp Jacobs L-4 engine and was the fourth production Staggerwing.

Below: YC-43 delivered for the use of the US Embassy in London in 1939.

Right: The final production Staggerwing model was the G17S, custom-built post-war at a cost of $29,000. This aircraft, the first production G17S, was sold in South America.

Below right: Olive Ann Beech, chief executive of Beech Aircraft, pictured with Staggerwing Club president 'Dub' Yarbrough and his G17S *Big Red*.

Kansas winds to smooth and fashion to perfection! Just sitting on the ground, leaning back like an eager greyhound, it looks as if it is going fast. But it is in the air, of course, that it is at its most beautiful.

Climb aboard through the single rear door and make your way up the sloping floor to the cockpit, heavy with the scent of old aeroplane, a blend of leather, oil, gasoline, dope and a whiff of the past. And all that room! A wide bench seat for three in the back, and individual seats up front. Beech even used to offer special seats with built-in parachutes, presumably for those of a nervous disposition. The cockpit is pure 1930s, haphazardly arranged with cranks, levers, wheels, taps and knobs placarded with varying degrees of instruction, caution, advice and consolation, and a big half-moon shaped control wheel mounted on Beech's familiar 'throwover' arm so that the aeroplane may be flown from either seat.

You start a Pratt & Whitney Wasp in much the same way that I imagine steam traction engine enthusiasts fire up their machines: with a lot of

coaxing, a little cajoling, and perhaps a curse or two. But once off and running there is no sound that equals that of a Pratt & Whitney at take-off power. With 450 hp a yard ahead of your knees you do not attempt conversation. However, the noise quickly subsides as the retractable undercarriage comes up beneath the cabin floor and the Staggerwing loafs upward in a leisurely 1,000 feet per minute climb. It will go up to 26,000 feet or beyond – jet country – if you wish, where few ancient biplanes are seen (there's an aerial survey operator in the United States who uses one for his mapping business and regularly startles airliner crews when they spot him going past in the opposite direction, higher than they are) and cruise at 180 mph for five hours with five people and their baggage aboard, in comfort all too rare today, then land at tiny grass airstrips which many modern lightplanes could never get into.

When you do decide to land there is another delight in store. As you select landing gear *down*, from beneath your feet comes this clattering, chain-over sprockets rattle, clacking away like a

This pristine G17S is owned
by Jim Gorman of Mansfield,
Ohio.

ship dropping anchor or that delightful sound kids make with cigarette packets in the spokes of bicycle wheels. I have never timed this curious gear-lowering symphony, but it seems ages before the gear *down and locked* light blinks on, and I am sure that the sound alone would be sufficient reminder to lower the Staggerwing's wheels before landing. But if not, there is an interconnect mechanism which is supposed to prevent full closure of the throttle unless the undercarriage is lowered. Walter Beech used a specially adapted Model 17 (it had metal skids under its belly) to demonstrate how safe a gear-up landing could be during the 1930s. His salesmen would take a prospective customer for a ride, stop the engine with the propeller horizontal, then glide down to land without lowering the wheels. It must have been very reassuring, but it did not prevent real gear-up landings. And real damage.

What made the Staggerwing so special? Not just its unusual appearance. Performance, mostly. Its airframe design, now nearly half a century old, is so clean that even after an engine failure (despite the old saying about *Trust in God and Pratt & Whitney* – even The Almighty has been known to fail occasionally) the aircraft is reluctant to slow up, so that the pilot's manual recommends an immediate 500-foot *climb*, trading airspeed for altitude while you sort things out.

The immaculate handling of the Staggerwing could easily dupe you into thinking that it was designed as a fighter. Its finger-light ball-bearing hinged control surfaces demand no more than a hint, a suggestion of what you would like them to do for the aeroplane to obey. Flying it is a rare delight. The Beechcraft, Model 17. Name it what you will, whatever you call it, Staggerwing spells *style*.

STRINGBAG

'Would you like to help start her up?' they asked. But I knew about Pegasus engines, they have inertia starters whose heavy flywheels must be spun up to very high speeds by plug-in hand-cranks, and it is hard, exhausting work, so I left it to the ground crew. Cheeks puffed, faces scarlet going on puce, they cranked ever faster as if winding the ultimate clockwork toy. It must have taken two minutes or more of frantic, arm-jellifying cranking to get the 'Peggy' firing. What can it have been like on the pitching deck of an aircraft carrier?

The occasion was a rare and treasured flight in the Royal Navy's beloved Stringbag, a Fairey Swordfish torpedo bomber. The nickname Stringbag, incidentally, is not, as you might suppose, a reference to the confusion of bracing wires which seem to hold the Swordfish together, but stems from a passing remark made about the biplane's extraordinary load-carrying abilities. 'No housewife on a shopping spree could cram a wider variety of articles into her string bag,' the man said, and Stringbag it has been ever since.

The Swordfish was an anacronism from the start, a design dating back to a 1932 specification which not only entered service long after other naval air arms were committed to monoplanes for torpedo bombing but outlasted its intended successor, the Albacore (another anacronism),

and ultimately was responsible for the sinking of a greater tonnage of enemy shipping than any other Allied aircraft.

The Swordfish, then designated TSR II (for Torpedo-Spotter-Reconnaissance, and not to be confused with the later TSR.2 supersonic bomber) was designed by a team led by Fairey Aviation's Belgian chief designer Marcel Lobelle, a man not noted for innovation, though a highly competent aircraft designer. The prototype flew from Fairey's Great West Aerodrome, where now stands London-Heathrow Airport, on 17 April 1934. A year later a contract was awarded for production machines, now named Swordfish, to operate off Royal Navy aircraft carriers in torpedo-bombing and reconnaissance roles. Paradoxically the Swordfish order was placed in the same month that prototypes of a radical new torpedo bomber monoplane, the Blackburn Skua, were commissioned. One can only suppose that the Admiralty adopted a belt-and-braces policy, ordering the tried-and-tested formula employed in Swordfish design lest the modern design should have unforeseen shortcomings, which it did.

In total 2,391 Swordfish were built, virtually all wartime production coming from the Blackburn plant at Sherburn-in-Elmet, Yorkshire while Fairey's Hayes, Middlesex factory concentrated on the Albacores which were supposed to replace them. Despite the Albacore's enclosed, heated cockpits they were never popular among Fleet Air Arm pilots, giving rise to this ditty sung to the tune of 'My Bonny Lies Over the Ocean':

The Swordfish relies on her Peggy,
The modified Taurus ain't sound,
So the Swordfish flies off on her missions,
And the Albacore stays on the ground.
Bring back, oh bring back,
Oh bring back my Stringbag to me.

The trusty 'Peggy' was a nine-cylinder Bristol Pegasus radial engine, rated at 750 hp in later versions of the Swordfish, and driving a three-

blade Fairey Reed propeller of nearly 12-foot diameter, as might befit a biplane which stands almost as tall as a bus. The Swordfish's airframe was all metal: welded steel tube fuselage with alclad skinning and armour plate on the forward section, fabric to the rear, with fabric covered wings and tail surfaces. Mark II Swordfish had metal underskinning on their strengthened lower wings with weapons hard points for rocket launchers. The Stringbag, like its namesake, could carry a prodigious load of stores, pushing its empty weight of 4,700 pounds to an operational overload gross of almost double that at 9,250 pounds. It was almost impossible to overload and no matter what was slung beneath its fuselage or wings, the Swordfish's performance, modest though it was, remained virtually unchanged and always predictably reliable. It could be pulled off a carrier deck at 55 knots and thrown into a tight climbing turn with no fear of stalling and spinning. In a strong wind a Swordfish would be off the deck the instant its throttle was opened. Those operating off the very short decks of MAC-ships (Merchant Aircraft Carriers) were equipped with RATOG (Rocket-Assisted Take-Off Gear) tubes for near helicopter-like performance.

So simple to fly was the Stringbag that it was widely used to give pilots their first experiences of catapult launching, even when they had never flown the aircraft before, and its slow speed stability made it a natural for practising the difficult art of carrier deck landing. Though abysmally slow the Swordfish's impeccable

Left: Torpedo slung beneath the Royal Navy Historic Flight's airworthy Swordfish serves as a baggage container for ferry flights to airshow appearances. Right: The Swordfish could carry a prodigious load of stores, almost doubling its empty weight in operational overload conditions, yet it remained easy and forgiving to fly. Note slats on upper wing contributing to its remarkable slow speed performance.
Above: Hook down in deck-landing configuration, the sole airworthy Fairey Swordfish makes a slow fly-by during an airshow performance.

manoeuvrability at low airspeeds and altitudes could, when properly exploited, be used to its advantage even against high performance enemy aircraft, making the apparently lumbering biplane much less of an easy prey than it looked. During the Norwegian campaign Fleet Air Arm pilots flying Swordfish would lure Luftwaffe fighter pilots up narrow fjords from which the faster machines were unable to escape, while the Stringbags could be racked around in tight turns right up against the fjord sides. Several Luftwaffe fighters were destroyed in this fashion without a shot being fired. A Swordfish floatplane catapulted from HMS *Warspite* was also instrumental in directing the ship's gunfire to destroy seven German destroyers in Ofot Fjord before dive bombing a U-Boat, the first one to be sunk by the Fleet Air Arm in the Second World War.

There was a popular (and possibly accurate) joke among Stringbag crews which alleged that the aircraft's routine cruise speed of 90 mph was slower than the minimum speed settings on German ships' anti-aircraft gunsights, and that it was therefore impossible for gunners to hit an aircraft except by chance, and then it would

likely be one flying *ahead* of the intended target. But there was one point in a Swordfish's mission when it was totally and mercilessly vulnerable – on the run in for a torpedo attack. The standard torpedo technique was to dive on the target near vertically. Even from 10,000 feet the drag-ridden airframe would hold the speed below 200 knots. Leaving the pull-out as late as possible the Swordfish pilot would then run in sighting the target with a clever device comprising two rods fixed to the upper wings trailing edge on which equally-spaced light bulbs were arranged so that the distance between each represented five knots of an enemy ship's speed. The delivery run, at precisely 60 feet above the waves, would be made at right angles to the ship, keeping the appropriate bulb aligned with it and avoiding any temptation to weave or dodge lethal anti-aircraft fire for fear of throwing the torpedo off line at the release point.

Loaded with its 18-inch, 1,610 pound torpedo, 1,500 pound mine or equivalent bomb load on under-wing racks the Swordfish had a 540-mile range, but for reconnaissance work this could be extended to 1,030 miles by a ventral tank, or in the offensive role by an overload tank with the crew reduced to two to accommodate the tank in the observer's position. The November 1940 attack on the Italian Fleet at Taranto, for which the Stringbag will forever be remembered, was almost ruined before it started when a fitter aboard HMS *Illustrious* dropped his screwdriver while installing one of these tanks, causing a spark which exploded the petrol laden atmosphere in the below decks hangar, destroying two Swordfish and damaging several others. The entire complement of aircraft was soaked with sea water from the ship's fire-control hoses and had to be taken up on deck and washed down with fresh water, each and every engine and instrument being stripped, cleaned and re-assembled overnight, in heavy seas. Somehow they managed it and subsequently *Illustrious'* Swordfish destroyed much of the Italian fleet (and all of their morale) in a surprise attack which set a precedent for the Japanese raid on Pearl Harbor. Only two Stringbags were lost despite taking more than 13,000 rounds of fire from Italian shore batteries.

At Narvik, Cape Matapan, the destruction of the *Bismarck*, even in the Western Desert — where one pilot loaded his Stringbag with 2,500 pounds of bombs and took 11 miles to get off the sand — the Swordfish gained a rare charisma and became a legend. Its role as torpedo bomber ended in 1942 after the catastrophic attempt to prevent the break-out of the German battleships *Scharnhorst*, *Gneisenau* and *Prinz Eugen* from Brest Harbour in appalling weather. Six Swordfish from 825 Squadron led by Lieutenant Commander Eugene 'Winkle' Esmonde heroically

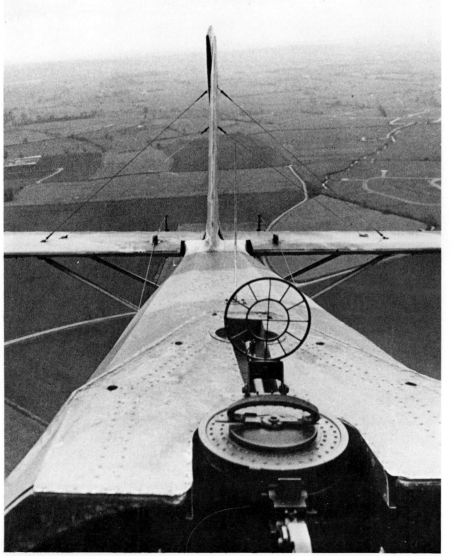

The telegraphist/air gunner's view from the icy 'bathtub' open cockpit of the Fleet Air Arm Historic Flight's Swordfish.

attacked the ships without fighter cover and were cut to pieces by ships' gunfire and by Luftwaffe fighters whose pilots flew with undercarriages and flaps down to keep pace with the sluggardly biplanes. All six were destroyed, only three crewmen survived and not a single torpedo struck home. For leading this futile action Esmonde was posthumously awarded the Victoria Cross. His bravery is in no doubt. What is questionable is the decision to mount such a suicidal attack.

Thereafter the Swordfish performed its greatest work as reconnaissance spotter, coastal patrol bomber, minelayer and, with ASV radar and rockets, as submarine hunter-killer. In the midst of the action from the outset, it was appropriate that a Swordfish from 119 Squadron Coastal Command flew the last recorded operation of the war, attacking a midget submarine in the English Channel four hours before the German surrender.

My impression of the Stringbag? *Cold!* The open three-man crew compartment forms an effective scoop which grabs every icy bladeful of air thrown back by the faithful Peggy's propeller. I froze on a mild April day. Imagine the cruel discomforts of those who flew these aeroplanes far out over the Atlantic from small merchantmen whose living quarters were as cramped as their cockpits, tormented by stomach disorders from bad food. Or those who operated Stringbags north to the Arctic Circle where raw winds savaged crews who, through administrative blunders, were never issued with the fleece-lined flying suits which their colleagues, snug in the enclosed heated cockpits of Blackburn Skuas, had. Exhausted by endless hours of duty, stiff and numb from the unyielding cold, the pilots would fall asleep at the controls, to be woken by hearty thumps from their observers whose tiny cubicles, cluttered with parachute, chart board, pro-

tractors, dividers, course-and-speed calculator, Wilkinson Computer, pencils and erasers, were scarcely conducive to peaceful slumber. With frozen fingers the observers struggled to take drift sightings through the iced-up perspex window in the floor beneath their camp-stool seat, or fought the slipstream to take compass bearings, dead-reckoning across tens of thousands of square miles of featureless unfriendly ocean, often in darkness, to find their way back to the insignificant specks of floating steel which were their homes. The flavour of those times is captured in this parody of Rudyard Kipling's 'If', composed for the inspiration of trainee Swordfish observers, the 'O Types':

If you can keep your track when all about you
Are losing theirs and setting mag for true;
If you can trust yourself when pilots doubt you,
And get back to the ship out of the blue;
If you can keep control of your dividers
And Bigsworth Board and Gosport Tube and
*   pad;*
Or listen to the wireless and the pilot
Talking in unison – and not go mad . . .
If you can fill the unforgiving minute
With sixty seconds' worth of ground speed run,
Your's is the Air, and everything that's in it,
And what is more, you'll be an 'O', my son.

They were heroes, there's no doubt. And the old Stringbag was a heroine. Not the 'long lean monarchs of the sky, that pilots would be proud to fly' described by one over-enthusiastic wartime poet. Stringbags were hardly long and lean. But he was right about pride. The Swordfish inspired in those who flew it an undying loyalty to an aeroplane that would never let you down, would take all the punishment that you could, and more, and bring you safely home again – alive, but cold.

In a strong breeze operational Swordfish could safely be lifted off a carrier's deck at 55 knots thanks to impeccable slow speed handling even at high gross weights.

YELLOW PERIL

The cattle town of Wichita, Kansas, seems an unlikely claimant to the title 'Aviation Capital of the World'. But its claim to the name dates back as far as 1919, when a rich oil wildcatter by the name of Jake Moellendick put up $30,000, with his partner Billy Burke, to persuade a gifted young aircraft designer called Matty Laird to move his company there from Chicago.

Laird brought with him a group of unknown but talented aircraft men: Buck Weaver, who later set up the Waco concern; Walter Beech; and Lloyd Carlton Stearman, a former architectural student and naval aviator, who went to work as a mechanic on Laird's Swallow biplanes. The group stayed together for several years building Swallows and losing money. Burke and Weaver both departed in 1922. In September 1923 Matty Laird took $1,500 and two Swallows and returned to Illinois after a dispute with Moellendick, and the company was reorganised as the Swallow Airplane Manufacturing Company with Beech as chief test and demonstration pilot and Lloyd Stearman as design engineer. Stearman's first task was to redesign the Swallow as a more compact single-bay biplane. Hardly had production begun on this New Swallow when Beech and Stearman also fell out with Moellendick over their plan to substitute welded steel tube for the aircraft's wooden fuselage, and they too departed to set up in business with a Kansas farmer and barnstormer named Clyde Cessna as the Travel Air Manufacturing Company, building Stearman's designs.

In 1926 Stearman moved west to Venice, California to form his own Stearman Aircraft Incorporated. His first biplane was the Stearman C-1, a 90 hp Curtiss OX-5 engined machine which carried two passengers seated side-by-side in the open front cockpit. Soon he substituted war surplus 240 hp Salmson engines for the OXs, and later a 200 hp Wright J-4. The motto 'Dedicated To The Discriminating Buyer' became a Stearman trademark, and one of the first such discriminating customers was Walter Varney, whose airline flew mail contracts between Salt Lake City and Seattle.

Stearman's company was under capitalised, and at that time California lacked visionary businessmen with money to invest in what appeared to be a shaky venture. Within a year he had moved back to Wichita, establishing a factory north of the town at Bridgeport, in the same building which Clyde Cessna had used to build his first aeroplane a decade before. It was 1927, the year of Lindbergh and business boomed. The first Wichita Stearmans were C-3MB mailplanes for Varney Air Lines and American Airlines. A whole series of Stearman C-3 biplanes followed, powered variously by Hisso, Comet, Siemens-Halske, Salmson and Wright engines. Top of the line was the 1929 model C-3R Business Speedster, powered by a 225 hp Wright motor. It sold for $8,000. Seven

'Missing man' formation
flown by a Waco Taperwing
and three 450 hp Stearmans
in honour of American
airshow pilot and announcer
Nick Rezich.

Right: Lloyd Stearman.

Below: Boeing-Stearman 'Kaydets' pictured over Kansas in 1942. Top to bottom: Peruvian PT-17, Canadian PT-27, Chinese PT-17, US Navy N2S-3 and US Army PT-17.

Far right: A PT-17 for China being test flown at Wichita prior to delivery.

Below right: Royal Canadian Air Force PT-27.

Stearman M-2 mailplanes, officially known as Speedmails, but colloquially referred to as 'Bull Stearmans' were built, and three transport versions with fully-enclosed four-seat cabins were delivered to Interstate Air Lines in June 1929.

Three months later Stearman Aircraft became part of the United Aircraft and Transport Corporation, a giant conglomerate which included Boeing, Hamilton-Standard, Pratt & Whitney, Sikorsky, United Airlines and Vought. Soon afterwards the Depression decimated the American aircraft industry, but Stearman opened a new factory adjacent to Wichita Municipal Airport, and Northrop Aircraft of Burbank, California merged with the company, its advanced all-metal monoplanes being marketed briefly as 'Stearman-Northrops', though none was actually built at Wichita. Simultaneously Stearman left the company which he had founded

but no longer controlled, to join up with his best customer Walter Varney, before becoming president of Lockheed aircraft in 1932.

Ironically it was not until after Stearman's departure that the biplane for which his name is best remembered (he died in April 1975) first appeared. And more surprisingly, he played no part in its design, though when it flew in December 1933 the Stearman Model 70 bore obvious signs of its lineage. In the following spring 61 aircraft were ordered for the US Navy and export variants went to the Philippine and Cuban governments. A developed Model X75 was selected by the US Army as a primary trainer in October 1934, to be designated PT-13. The PT-13 took on the shape which was to become familiar to every trainee American pilot in the Second World War and is synonymous with the name Stearman: uncowled radial engine, big tandem open cockpits, N-braced biplane wings, and a massive long-stroke undercarriage to cushion the shock of students' landings. Though it was, and is, called simply a 'Stearman', the PT-13 and its successors were actually Boeing aeroplanes, Boeing Aircraft Company having taken on the Stearman Division of United Aircraft as a wholly-owned subsidiary when a US Government antitrust ruling separated United's airline and manufacturing activities in September 1934. The PT-13 was also the first aircraft ever to meet the requirements of both Army and Navy, indeed some said it was the first time the rival services had ever been able to agree about *anything.*

In all 10,346 PT-13s, PT-17s, Navy N2Ss and Canadian Kaydets were delivered, including numerous sub-types. Most plentiful were the 220 hp Continental-engined PT-17s for the US Army and N2S-1s and 4s for the Navy. At any US Army training base in the early 1940s they would be lined up almost as far as the eye could see in serried ranks, chrome yellow wings, blue fuselages, rudders striped red, white and blue like Old Glory, ranged with military precision, the points of their white star insignias exactly aligned.

Cadets would troop out to the rows with their instructors, to the biplane which was to be their aerial alma mater. They called it a PT, or maybe a Stearman or Kaydet. The Navy guys called theirs N2Ss, but they were usually known as *Yellow Perils* – yellow for the colour of their wings, perils because it was unwise to get too near one when it was being flown by a rookie pilot to whom it was a classroom. Though it was a biplane, and not at all like the sleek new fighters they put on the recruiting posters, cadets were comforted to learn that no-one had ever succeeded in breaking a Stearman apart in the air. A bored Air Corps instructor did once put one into a terminal velocity dive, then suddenly pulled up, just to see if the wings would come off. They did

Far left: Stearmans are popular mounts for airshow performers. This sunburst-schemed biplane has a 450 hp Pratt & Whitney Wasp engine.

Centre left: Toe-hanging: Wayne Pierce making an inverted fly-by in his 450 hp Stearman *Ole Smokey* with wing-walker atop the centre section.

Left: The 220 hp Continental engine was standard on wartime Stearmans, like these two restored in US Army and US Navy markings.

Below: 'Yellow Peril': a Stearman beautifully restored in the colours of a US Navy N2S-3 trainer.

Sunbursts or chequers are *de rigueur* for airshow Stearmans like Wayne Pierce's *Ole Smokey*.

not, though the cadet in front went to pieces!

Instructors would do the oddest things when they were bored. They would climb from their cockpit, stand on the wingroot and suddenly tap a trainee on the shoulder at 5,000 feet. A popular trick played on nervous cadets was to slip the release pin on the instructor's control column and make a grand gesture of throwing the stick overboard. *OK son, now you've got to fly it.* One young trainee panicked and did the same thing with *his* stick. Fortunately his instructor was a wily old hand who always carried with him a short length of broom handle for just such an emergency. He inserted it into the empty socket, flew the Stearman home and sent the cadet back by road to search for the discarded control columns.

When the war ended so began the Stearman's second career. Thousands of surplus military trainers came on the civil market at a few hundred dollars apiece, and the Stearman formed the backbone of America's agricultural aviation fleet. The rugged airframe designed by Boeing-Wichita's Harold Zipp and Jack Clark proved readily adaptable to more powerful engines and heavy chemical hoppers in place of the front cockpit. The people of America owe a great debt to the Stearman for its role in crop treatment. It was the corner stone of an industry, and is still a favourite mount of crop-dusting pilots. Gordon Baxter, the aviation writer and Texas radio personality, is an unashamed Stearman fan. He and a group of his friends composed this little ditty (to be sung with tongue-in-cheek) at a party for Stearman ag pilots. He says he was never invited again:

Oh, the Stearman's a very fine airplane
Constructed of paper and wood
It's splendid for carrying whiskey
But for dusting it's strictly no good.

There's more to the Stearman than just an able workhorse, though. Since the war the biplane has become a favourite aerobatic mount for airshow pilots. With a 450 hp Pratt & Whitney engine (or even a 600 hp mill) a Stearman is a crowd-puller par excellence.

There is also a thriving trade in restored Stearmans. Antique aeroplane enthusiasts, many of whom first took to the air in Army PTs or Navy N2Ss, covet the old biplanes. Specialist restorers turn aged, chemical-stained cropdusters into pristine jewels with chrome-plated struts and propellers and hand-rubbed paint. A really good one might cost close to $100,000. In 1943 the US Army paid $9,120 for it. And that same blue and yellow colour scheme is still the most popular. There's no spending limit on nostalgia. And there is no aeroplane more likely to get an American pilot damp-eyed than a Stearman. Just don't ever call it a Boeing. They build big paraffin burning jets: a Stearman is a *real* aeroplane.

BOXKITES

'Like sitting on a jelly in a strong breeze,' replied the pioneer British aviator J. T. C. Moore-Brabazon (later Lord Brabazon of Tara) when asked what it was like to fly his Voisin biplane *Bird of Passage* in the spring of 1909. Brabazon was the recipient of the Royal Aero Club's British Aviator's Certificate No. 1, having made the first flight by a Briton from British soil that year. He was also the man who confounded the old saying 'when pigs fly' by taking a squealing piglet for a ride on the wing of his machine.

The Voisin which he flew was the first viable European aeroplane (and, incidentally, it was also the type of machine on which the world's first woman pilot, Baroness Raymonde de Laroche, was taught to fly), the creation of the brothers Charles and Gabriel Voisin. Gabriel drew up plans for his first flying machine in 1900, and in later years he and his brother experimented with gliders and collaborated with Louis Blériot and the French industrialist and enthusiastic supporter of early aviators Ernest Archdeacon, for whom *Les Frères Voisin* of Billancourt, near Paris, constructed a boxkite floatplane glider (or hydroplane as it was then styled) which made a successful flight of some 600 metres under motor-boat tow along the River Seine in June 1905.

The 1905 glider was the inspiration for two powered biplanes built in 1907 for Henri Farman (who, despite his name was an Englishman domiciled in France) and for Léon Delagrange. The cellular boxkite principle was adopted for both wings and tail surfaces, the wings of the aircraft divided into separate cells by 'side curtains', with a biplane forward elevator, but no form of lateral control whatever, Voisin being a firm believer in the principle of inherent stability despite the pioneering work on wing-warping which had been done by the Wrights, whose efforts and achievements he continued to denigrate with inexhaustible vitriol for more than 60 years.

The Voisin-Delagrange (Voisin named his aircraft after his customers) was completed and ready for flight on 20 February 1907, and taken to Vincennes where it was to be demonstrated to its new owner as a condition of the purchase, the Voisins having been given 25 per cent of the price in advance, the balance due when the aircraft flew without accident. Charles Voisin started the 50 hp Antoinette engine . . . and the aeroplane broke in two.

A week later it was ready again, and again it broke. Another week, and once more the Voisin was prepared, this time at the military parade

Below, right and overleaf: The Shuttleworth Trust's Bristol Boxkite replica was built for the film *Those Magnificent Men in Their Flying Machines.*

ground at Bagatelle, in the Bois de Boulogne. 'I started the engine towards eleven in the morning,' Gabriel wrote later. 'Charles rolled for 100 feet and then moved the elevator for climb. The machine left the ground, completed a flight of about 260 feet at a height of thirteen to sixteen feet and returned to earth without incident.' M. Delagrange promptly handed over the money, which was badly needed, the Voisins' meagre cash reserves having been almost completely absorbed by wage bills, the purchase of materials and their outstanding account at the local bistro near the company premises in rue de la Ferme.

It was to there that Henri Farman came in May 1907. A former racing cyclist and car driver, he wanted an aeroplane with which to compete for the 50,000 franc prize put up by Ernest Archdeacon and Henri Deutsch de la Meurthe for the first pilot to complete a one kilometre closed-circuit without incident. Farman was not an aviator, but then at the time neither was anyone else in Europe. By October 1907 he was flying the Voisin, and on 9 November he flew a distance of 1,030 metres, remaining in the air for 74 seconds – the longest that any aeroplane other than a Wright Flyer had sustained itself at that time.

On 12 January 1908 Farman gave members of the Aero Club de France's distinguished committee the required 24 hours notice of a proposed attempt at the Deutsch-Archdeacon Prize and next day successfully negotiated the one kilometre course in 1 minute and 28 seconds, causing

the normally staid Aero Club officials to fling their hats in the air as he passed the marker flag at the end of the course. 'At this moment none of our competitors was worrying us,' crowed Gabriel Voisin in triumph, 'We were indeed the only people in the world able to offer an aeroplane capable of flying more or less correctly, and although an army of plagiarists tried their best to equal us, not one could claim to approach the results we obtained.' Except the Wright brothers, who by this time had made flights up to 24 miles.

The triumphant Voisin machine had, in fact, been so modified by its owner that the medal which the Voisin brothers received attesting to the quality of their flying machines was only just deserved. Henri Farman had replaced the bi-plane front elevator with a monoplane surface and given the wings dihedral to improve the aircraft's lateral stability. Voisin later adopted the single-surface elevator on his aircraft, though he remained true to the square boxkite rig of his wings. Farman continued to develop the design and market it under his own name, laying himself open to regular lashings from Gabriel's sharp tongue.

For several years after the Deutsch-Archdeacon triumph the Voisin and Farman designs had a profound influence on the development of European aviation and were widely copied and produced under licence. The Bristol Boxkite, which was the first commercially produced British aeroplane, was a licence-manufactured version of a Farman design. Unlike the Voisins it did have lateral controls in the form of ailerons on upper and lower wings. The foreplane elevator and biplane tail surfaces with triple rudders were retained. Pilot and passenger sat in the open on the centre-section of the lower wing ahead of a 50 hp Gnôme rotary engine driving a pusher propeller. A young army captain named Sefton Brancker, later to become famous as the Director of Civil Aviation and champion of private flying, took part in early trials to assess the Boxkite's military potential. He recalled it as 'not a particularly comfortable conveyance . . . a mass of light spars, piano wire and fabric which responded to every change of temperature (*this was in India*) and as the nights were very cold with a heavy dew, while the sun by day was burning hot, the spars bowed, wires stretched and contracted, fabric sagged and the whole structure creaked and cracked as if it were going to fall to pieces.' Poor Brancker tried to make artillery observations and draw sketches while aloft on this contraption.

Another unfortunate passenger, a woman, who rode on a Farman at Rheims in 1909 remarked: 'How I got up I do not know, and what I sat on I do not comprehend. I was only conscious that the pilot, when he scrambled in after me, was very close in front, wedging me in tightly between himself and the radiator of the engine behind. I was his first passenger, of either sex, and passenger flight had not been contemplated or arranged for. One word of warning he conveyed to me – not to touch his arms . . . We tore along at an increasing pace that was very soon greater than any motor I had yet been in . . . and then!, suddenly there had come into it a new indescribable quality, a lift, a lightness, a life! Very many there are now who know that feeling, that glorious, gliding sense that the sea-bird has known this million years, and which man has so long and so vainly envied it . . . but picture if you can what it meant for the *first* time, when all the world of aviation was fresh and untried, when to rise at all was a glorious adventure . . .'.

THE GIANTS FROM ST. PETERSBURG

The biennial aviation jamboree known as the Paris Air Show was, in the 1960s and early 1970s, the stage for a curious game of cold war one-upmanship between the Soviet Union and the United States. At almost every show there would be a tantalising gap in the schedule of Russian exhibits for an 'unspecified' aircraft, about which ill-informed speculation would run rife. In 1971 the Americans brought along their immense Lockheed C-5A Galaxy military transport jet, which is the world's largest operational aircraft. They obviously felt confident that the Russians would never be able to top that. But they did, for the Soviet Union's 'unspecified aircraft' that year was a Mil V-12 helicopter. It was not as big as the C-5A but as helicopters go it was gargantuan.

The world's first very large aircraft also came from Russia. In 1912, Igor Sikorsky, later to become famous for his pioneering work in helicopter development and for the formation of the American company which bears his name, ate dinner with a Mr. Shidlovsky, chairman of the Society of Russian Baltic Railroad Car Factories, in whose St. Petersburg works Sikorsky was

building small single-engine biplanes. During the course of their meal Sikorsky confided to Shidlovsky his plan to build a revolutionary kind of aeroplane, with four engines and a fully-enclosed passenger cabin. Over black coffee they discussed how such a machine might carry commercial passengers, how the cabin would provide protection in the harsh Russian climate, how the stability of such a large aeroplane would even

Above: Igor Sikorsky.

Right: Sikorsky's splendid *Le Grand*. Note the open balcony and searchlight.

Imperial Russian Air Service Ilia Mourometz heavy bomber.

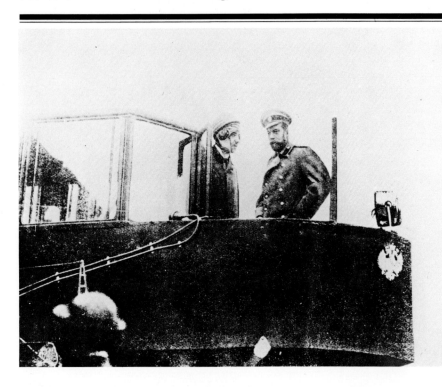

used on heavy jet airliners today, but with central skids in case the bogies failed. The cabin area was novel, and looked as if it owed as much to the Baltic Company's railway carriage experience as to aeronautical practice. At the front was a large open balcony with a searchlight mounted on a gimbal. Within, a dual-control cockpit, and behind this a luxurious passenger compartment with four seats, a sofa and a table, washroom, and a closet for passengers' coats. 'It was like something out of Jules Verne, though not so impractical,' Sikorsky observed.

The *Le Grand* flew on the evening of 13 May, Sikorsky having first assured Shidlovsky that he

Right and left: Sikorsky (*left*) and Emperor Nicholas II inspecting *Le Grand* at Krasnoe Selo, July 1913.

Below: A famous shot of the first *Ilia Mourometz* landing with two nonchalant strollers on top of its fuselage 'promenade'.

enable mechanics to work on its engines in flight. Shidlovsky, unlike so many contemporary experts who claimed that one ton was the maximum practical weight for an aeroplane, was spellbound, and as Sikorsky left his home he advised him: 'Start construction immediately'.

By November 1912 the giant aeroplane was well under way, the urgency of the project heightened by increasing scepticism outside the Baltic Company's factory. One helpful soul observed to Sikorsky that since nature's flying creatures were mostly several hundred times lighter than their earthbound counterparts, he was flying (or rather would *not* be flying) in the face of God; his aeroplane would run along the ground but it would not take to the air, it would be like the ostrich. Another opined that flying an aeroplane was like riding a motor bicycle, and thus attempting to fly a large machine would be like building an omnibus with only two wheels.

The aeroplane was completed in May 1913, and Sikorsky named it *Le Grand* (post-Czarist Russian publications also refer to it as the *Bolshoi* or *Russkii Vitiaz* – Russian Knight). It weighed 9,000 pounds loaded, had a wingspan of 92 feet, and was powered by four 100 hp four cylinder water-cooled Argus engines, set out between the biplane wings. Still the critics warned Sikorsky of his folly, finally resorting to the old fear that a pilot would not be able to judge his attitude in an enclosed cabin because of the absence of wind on his face. One may scoff at the doubters, but barely a decade after the Wright brothers' first flight, and just a few years after the first powered flights in Europe, *Le Grand* was a monumental undertaking, in all senses. Some problems were very basic: no wheels of adequate size could be obtained, so a 16-wheel bogie undercarriage had to be constructed, just like those

had no superstition over the date, and made a faultless and incident free flight to an altitude of 800 feet and a duration of eight minutes, after which Sikorsky and his mechanics (who had gone along as ballast and had intended to move swiftly about the cabin to trim the aircraft if needed, which they were not) stepped onto the aircraft's balcony to take the applause from a crowd of thousands of spectators ringing the airfield. During the summer of 1913 *Le Grand* made 53 flights, including one of 1 hour 53 minutes' duration with eight people aboard, and much valuable information was gained on the characteristics of multi-engined aircraft, for this was the world's first successful four-engined aeroplane and the first purpose-designed airliner. It was destroyed in August 1913 when a military Voisin biplane broke up in the air, and its engine crashed through the wing of *Le Grand* while it was parked on the airfield.

Sikorsky had already begun work on an even bigger machine, the *Ilia Mourometz*, (named after a tenth-century folk-hero), which not only had a balcony once again, but an upper bridge, cabin heating and lighting and a promenade along the top of the rear fuselage. The first flight was delayed because Sikorsky, anticipating a typically harsh St. Petersburg winter, had installed a ski undercarriage. However, the weather in January 1914 was mild, the snow melted, and no wheel landing gear was ready, so he attempted a take-off from the wet grass on the skis, and flew the machine for just long enough to ascertain that it was tail heavy. Modifications improved the *Ilia Mourometz*'s handling and numerous flights were made, including a record trip on 11 February 1914 carrying 16 passengers – and a dog. A familiar picture of the *Ilia Mourometz* shows it descending for a landing with two fur-hatted passengers nonchalantly taking a stroll along the promenade deck. A second aircraft was built with 140 hp engines at the inboard stations and 125 hp motors to outboard. This *Mourometz* carried seven people aloft on a duration flight which lasted for 6 hours and 33 minutes, and made a 1,600 mile flight from St. Petersburg to Kiev, inspiring the Imperial Russian Army to place an order for ten aircraft. In all 73 were eventually built for military use as heavy bombers and proved so successful on more than 400 raids against Germany and Lithuania during 1915 that the governments of Great Britain and France sought Czar Nicholas II's permission to licence-build the *Ilia Mourometz*, though nothing came of the idea before the 1917 Revolution which sent Sikorsky into exile in the United States, there to continue a brilliant career in aviation. Poor Shidlovsky, whose visionary encouragement had enabled Sikorsky to create the world's first successful multi-engined aircraft, was shot by the revolutionaries.

GOOD SCOUTS

The Sopwith Aviation Company's works must at times have seemed like a zoo – a quick check of their prodigious output in eight years of production reveals an Antelope, Bat, Bee, Buffalo, Camel, Cuckoo, Dolphin, Dove, Dragon, Grasshopper, Hippo, Rhino, Salamander, Snail, Snipe, Swallow, Wallaby, and even a Gnu. Funnily enough, however, the Sopwith Pup, so frequently characterised as 'the perfect flying machine', was known officially and unromantically as the Sopwith Type 9901 Scout. The origin of the name 'Pup' is obscure, but is allegedly attributed to Sefton Brancker, who observed that the Type 9901 resembled 'a 1½ Strutter's Pup'.

In fact the Pup owed less to the classic 1½ Strutter than it did to another uninspiringly named Sopwith, the SL.T.B.P., which was built for Harry Hawker, one of the Sopwith company's founders, as a personal runabout in 1915. Herbert Smith, whose task it was to put Harry Hawker's sketchy ideas of aircraft onto paper, reworked the SL.T.B.P. as a single-seat scout powered by an 80 hp Le Rhône rotary engine, and the first Type 9901 emerged from the Sopwith experimental shop on 9 February 1916. The name Pup was fiercely resisted in official circles, not least at The Admiralty, who were Sopwith's first customers for the aircraft, but it soon fell into such common use that all hope of persuading pilots to adopt the Type 9901 designation had to be abandoned. The Pup was a new breed of fighting machine: trim and very light (it weighed just 787 pounds empty), so that its modest 80 hp could

still extract a top speed of 111 mph from the aircraft. Light wing loading and a good power to weight ratio gave it excellent high altitude manoeuvrability, even close to its service ceiling of 17,500 feet. Where other scouts would become sluggish and unresponsive, the little Pup would continue to put on its agile, heel-snapping performance.

Its failings were a dismally small windscreen set into the butt of its single synchronised .303 Vickers machine-gun, and the armament itself. A single gun was inadequate firepower even in those early months of 1916, and the Vickers was uncommonly prone to jamming, especially in the cold air at high altitudes, leaving the Pup pilot with no weapon save for the aeroplane's superior manoeuvrability, which could be used to advantage in out-turning an enemy and making a rapid dive (but not too rapid – pilots reported that the Pup's wings started to flap at much more than 160 mph) for the British lines. Pilots from 54 Squadron, Royal Flying Corps, the first RFC unit to fly Pups, offered this musical advice in such circumstances:

When you soar in the air in your Sopwith Scout,
And you're scrapping with a Hun and your gun
· cuts out,
Well, you stuff down your nose till your plugs
fall out,
'Cos you haven't got a hope in the morning!

Below and Right: The 1913 Sopwith Tabloid was designed as a light, high performance sporting and military scout aircraft. With an 80 hp Gnome rotary engine it had a maximum speed of 92 mph which was remarkable for its day. Sopwith pilot Howard Pixton flew a 100 hp seaplane Tabloid to victory in the 1914 Schneider Trophy Race at Monaco at an average speed of 86.78 mph, and set a new world speed record

Factory profile of an 80 hp
Le Rhône-engined Sopwith
Pup, handsomely turned-out
with machine-turned engine
cowling.

That was sung to the tune of 'D'ye Ken John Peel'. Fifty-Four, who seem to have been an especially musical crowd, also composed this unsubtle warning to German fliers when first they received their Pups, to the tune of 'We've Come Up From Somerset':

Oh, we've come up from Fifty-four,
We're the Sopwith Pups you know,
And wherever you dirty swine may be
The Sopwith Pups will go.
And if you want a proper scrap,
Don't chase 2C's any more,
For we'll come up and do the job,
Because we're Fifty-four.

The Pup first entered service with 8 Squadron, Royal Naval Air Service on the Western Front in the winter of 1916/17, and was soon blooded. 'Naval Eight' destroyed 14 German aircraft in their first three months of action, and despite its low power and inadequate armament the Pup retained British dominance of the skies for the first half of 1917. A 54 Squadron pilot noted: 'Our best chances came from climbing above the maximum height obtainable by the German fighters and then hoping to make a surprise attack. The Germans were always superior in level speed and in the dive, but the Pup was much more

manoeuvrable and we could turn inside a German fighter any day.' The Pup could even hold its own against the new Albatros DIII. James McCudden, Britain's fourth highest-scoring pilot of the war, and winner of a Victoria Cross, flew Pups in France with 66 Squadron RFC and observed that 'the Pup could out manoeuvre any Albatros no matter how good the German pilot was, and when it came to manoeuvring, the Sopwith could turn twice to the Albatros's once.' Baron Manfred von Richthofen admitted that

Above: Pups were tested with a variety of skid landing gears during deck-landing trials aboard Royal Navy vessels late in 1917.

'the enemy aeroplane was clearly superior' when his flight of Albatroses fought with a Pup in January 1917.

Pup pilots took pains to squeeze every foot of climb rate and altitude out of their aircraft to take maximum advantage of the Sopwith's performance at high levels, stripping them of all unnecessary weight. First to go was the heavy but inefficient windscreen, which did little to shield pilots from the slipstream or from the fine haze of castor oil which blew back from the Le Rhone. Some experienced hands claimed that liberal doses of Scotch whisky would ward off the undesirable effects of the castor oil; it would certainly have helped keep you warm.

To the Pup also went the task of proving the practicality of operating scouts from the decks of ships, to which the Sopwith aeroplane proved to be ideally suited. The first deck landing by any aeroplane on a ship while she was under way took place on 2 August 1917 when Squadron Commander E. H. Dunning landed his Pup on the specially-built forward flying deck of the light battle cruiser-cum-aircraft-carrier HMS *Furious* as she steamed at 26 knots. Five days later he repeated the performance, but on his third landing the Pup's engine failed to respond as he tried to counter a sudden gust and the aeroplane was blown into the sea, drowning Dunning. A much-published series of pictures of the trials shows deckhands clutching at the rope toggles on the Pup's wings (there was no form of arrester gear) as if it were some escaped canary.

The origins of the Sopwith F.1 Camel's name are similarly beset with controversy. Some will tell you that the humped fairing over the aircraft's twin .303 Vickers guns inspired the appellation. Others contend that the lack of dihedral on the craft's upper wing and the sharply-dihedralled lower ones gave it a hump-backed, round-shouldered appearance. However it got its name, there is no doubt that the first rumours of the Sopwith F.1's existence early in 1917 caused great excitement and anticipation in RFC messes. The rumours claimed that Sopwith had a new two-gun fighter with a 130 hp engine which could fly at 130 mph in level flight. The rumours were true, and in due course the Camel, like the Pup, earned affection from those who flew it, but in this case tempered with a healthy, cautious respect, for the Camel was no docile machine. It was to emerge the superlative combat aircraft of the Great War, with a claimed victory tally of 2,790 enemy aircraft in less than two years, yet if it was mishandled the Camel could be as lethal to its injudicious pilot as its twin Vickers guns could be to an opponent.

Both the Camel's superior combat performance and its antisocial pilot-biting behaviour stemmed from the manoeuvrability afforded by the concentration of all its main masses – pilot,

fuel tank, engine, guns and ammunition – in just seven feet of the forward fuselage. Combined with the strong gyroscopic forces of its rotary engine (most commonly the 130 hp Clerget, though Camels were also powered by 110 hp Le Rhône and 150 hp Bentley motors), this mass concentration made the Camel uniquely responsive in turns, but also highly sensitive to the extent that the aircraft's control surfaces were sometimes unable to counteract the strong forces resulting from careless piloting. While it was true that the Camel was 'the kind of aeroplane which could turn on a sixpence and give you fivepence ha'penny change', it would also short-change you given the opportunity. The Camel was unstable in all axes, which is no bad thing in an aerobatic aircraft or a fighter flown by skilled pilots. It thus had the makings of a fine dog-fighter and could make the speediest change of direction among its contemporaries. Such was the gyroscopic action of its spinning engine that turns in either direction required full *left* rudder. Going left against the gyro action of the motor was ponderously slow; going right, with the action, instant and snappy, a trap for the unwary. Many Camel pilots found that a 90 degree turn to the left could most quickly be made by going *right*

through 270 degrees. The need for firm and correct rudder control was vital in the Camel, and since the direction of control input was often the opposite of what seemed logical, many pilots found themselves spinning, especially if they made the mistake of suddenly opening up the rotating engine at low airspeed. The sudden burst of gyroscopic force would snap the Camel over in a trice. Little was known in the First World War about the true nature of the spin, or of the corrective measures to be taken to recover, and the Camel soon achieved notoriety as a killer.

The Camel's tendency to spin was equalled in squadron legend by its apparent inability to recover from inverted flight. Several fatalities occurred in Camels which dived to earth upside down and the word was spread that once inverted the aeroplane would stabilise with no hope of recovery. All 'stunting' was summarily banned and questions were asked in the House of Commons about the Camel's record. In time the truth emerged: the Camel's twitchy response in pitch

Above: A replica of the Sopwith Tabloid, a seaplane version of which won the 1914 Schneider Trophy Race at Monaco.

Left: Sir Thomas Sopwith.

had caught pilots unawares. A sudden forward movement on the stick brought such an instant response that a brief moment of negative g would catapult the pilot from his seat. Captain Roy Brown, who is credited with the shooting down of von Richthofen, was moved to observe that 'the spade handled stick is strong enough to hang onto if you get inverted' and a few lucky ones did manage to scramble back into the cockpits of their inverted Camels. The famous four-piece Sutton Harness solved the problem.

In the hands of a skilled pilot the Camel became a formidable hunting weapon which could be treated almost as an extension of his body, and unlike the Pup the Camel was not lacking in firepower. The two Vickers guns had 500 rounds of ammunition apiece, and a double gun jam was so rare an occurrence that Camel pilots seldom needed to run for friendly lines. One aircraft alone set a record for destroying German aircraft, that of Major William Barker VC, DSO, MC, a Canadian 'artist with a pair of Vickers' who kept his Camel even when commanding a Bristol

Fighter squadron and destroyed 33 aeroplanes and nine kite balloons with it, and had six other kills unconfirmed.

But the Camel was not just a killing machine. It was pure delight for the pilot who wanted to perform aerobatics, or 'Camelbatics' as the greatest exponent used to call it. He was Captain D. V. Armstrong, DFC, who flew with 78 Squadron at Sutton's Farm on the outskirts of London. Another exponent of the Camel, Major Oliver Stewart, MC, AFC, wrote of him: 'He specialised in loops from a relatively low speed from ground level . . . His flick-rolls were started at less than the height of the sheds, and it is recorded that on one occasion his wingtip brushed the grass as the aeroplane went round.' Armstrong lost his life two weeks before the war ended while attempting to roll his Camel through an open hangar.

To sum up Tommy Sopwith's scouts, what better way than to extend the animal analogy a little further. The Pup was a friendly, trustworthy mongrel; the Camel a highly-strung pedigree.

FORMIDABLE FOKKER

There was a clause in the terms of the Armistice agreement signed by Germany at the end of the First World War which ran: 'In the first place, all D.VII aeroplanes...'. That was the *Fokker* D.VII, and its significance may be judged from the knowledge that no other German aircraft was specifically named in the surrender document. As it transpired not all D.VIIs were handed over. Anthony Fokker swiftly emptied his factory at Schwerin of everything movable, including 220 aircraft (70 D.VIIs), more than 400 aero-engines and 100 parachutes, hid the lot in sheds and farm buildings and then took them in 350 goods wagon-loads across the border to his native Holland, from where he did a fine post-war trade selling the aircraft throughout Europe, and even back into Germany, aided by the German ace Herman Goering who briefly acted as sales agent until his taste for high-living ran too rich for Fokker's pocket.

However, back in the autumn of 1917 Fokker's Dr.I triplane was entering service, but was plagued with structural problems resulting from poor quality workmanship. The work was made good, but seeds of doubt had been sown in the minds of Germany's pilots, and the little triplane was destined to enjoy only a brief career. A competition for a new fighter had been arranged by the *Flugzeugmeisterei*, the winner to be decided by a testing committee of experienced combat pilots in a fly-off competition in January 1918. Fokker had been labouring under a severe disadvantage. Resenting his Dutch nationality his rival manufacturers had seen to it that supplies of the latest water-cooled Mercedes and BMW engines had been denied him, and he had been forced to use less efficient rotaries. The competition, however, specified that the competing designs should all be powered by the Mercedes engine, to make it as fair as possible. Fokker finally had his opportunity.

When the flight tests began on 18 January at Adlershof airfield, he presented no fewer than eight aeroplanes. One, the VII prototype, had been completed barely a few hours before the competition's deadline and had not been tested at all. When Fokker did fly it at Adlershof he quickly found out that it was unstable in pitch and yaw, had a vicious stall and would spin at the slightest provocation. Explaining that his newest machine had suffered 'a slight landing

No original Fokker D.VIIs are airworthy. This machine is a modern replica of Anthony Fokker's formidable fighter.

accident' he made an urgent telephone call to the factory at Schwerin summoning two of his best staff. They worked through the night – cut the fuselage in half, welded in a sixty centimetre extension, enlarged the VII's fin and rudder to correct the instability problems, and completed what was in effect an on the spot redesign just in time for Fokker to test the machine before it had to be handed over to the selection committee. It was better, but still very sensitive directionally. Turning adversity to advantage Fokker took one of the test pilots, Oberleutnant Bruno Loerzer, aside. 'You will observe something special about my aeroplane,' he let slip conspiringly. 'It responds very fast to control movements, and this makes it very manoeuvrable. Please tell your colleagues so that they can use this advice to their advantage.'

Having delivered his veiled warning Fokker went off in search of much-needed sleep and was duly rewarded not only with an unprecedented order for 400 of his aeroplanes, but with the sweet taste of revenge, for his rivals Albatros and AEG were also ordered to build the new Fokker machines. (AEG never did produce the Fokker D.VII, and Albatros's aircraft – manufactured after Fokker supplied a complete aeroplane as a pattern in the absence of any formal plans – were always thought to be better than those from the Schwerin factory, which was still suffering from quality control problems.)

As with the Dr.I triplane, much of the credit for the D.VII belongs rightly to Reinhold Platz, Fokker's chief designer, who had begun work as a welder and developed an intuitive talent for producing aeroplanes that performed spectacularly despite his having no formal training as an aircraft engineer and only the vaguest of briefs on each project from his employer. The D.VII continued the Fokker tradition of welded steel tube fuselages, but departed from the then-current fashion of thin airfoil sections in having a very thick wing section. The D.VII's wings had two box spars and their strength was legendary, tested to a load factor of 10.5 before they failed. There were no external bracing wires, just N-shaped interplane struts.

The thick wing gave the D.VII one of its most outstanding qualities: the ability to maintain very steep climbing angles, 'hanging on its propeller' without stalling, while its service ceiling of 6,000 metres gave it a good margin over the Sopwith Camel. A D.VII pilot could thus press home an attack while climbing below an enemy, or go above and dive on him. It was not fast (Fokker claimed a top speed of 124 mph, but Allied test pilots who flew captured D.VIIs thought 105 mph nearer the true figure) but it was formidably manoeuvrable and could be whipped around very tightly (remember the prototype's directional problems). The 160 hp Mercedes DIII six-cylinder inline was the finest German aero engine of the war.

The first Fokker D.VIIs were assigned to Manfred von Richthofen's *Jagdgeschwader* Nr.1 in the spring of 1918, two months after the prototype trials at Adlershof. Richthofen himself never flew the D.VII in combat, preferring his Dr.I triplane, but his successor Herman Goering was an enthusiastic exponent of the new Fokker, which he claimed was the finest German fighter of the war.

AEROPLANES FOR ALL

'My enthusiasm for natural history led me to seek the solution in entomology,' says the late Sir Geoffrey de Havilland in his autobiography *Sky Fever*. The problem which turned his mind to his great love of Lepidoptera was a name for a new biplane, the de Havilland D.H.60, which made its first flight from the London suburb of Stag Lane on 22 February 1925. 'It suddenly struck me,' Sir Geoffrey continues, 'that the name "Moth" was just right.' At the time he did not realise that the name Moth was not only *right*, but was destined to become a generic term for any light aeroplane among the British public in the 1920s and 1930s.

De Havilland's dream was of an aeroplane for all, a cheap, easy to fly, simple to operate machine which ordinary folk might use as a runabout much as they drove motor cars, an aeroplane to get the man and woman in the street into the air. Simplicity was the key to the Moth design: a plywood skinned box section fuselage with fabric-covered flying surfaces. The wings folded alongside the fuselage for storage or for towing home behind your automobile. The engine was a 60 hp ADC Cirrus four-cylinder inline, the creation of de Havilland's chief engineer Major Frank Halford from one half of a wartime surplus 120 hp Airdisco-Renault V-8 motor.

A week after its maiden flight the new Moth was demonstrated to the press at Stag Lane, where it was most enthusiastically received. 'Despite extremely bad aerodrome conditions, Mr. Broad *(de Havilland's famous test pilot Hubert Broad)* took a number of distinctly heavy

passengers into the air with extreme ease,' reported *The Aeroplane*. 'An Aeroplane for Youth,' proclaimed *The Times*, while the *London Press* described the Moth as 'the most practical and successful light aeroplane which the world has so far seen.' A convincing demonstration of the Moth's practicality came on 29 May 1925 when Alan Cobham flew the prototype from Croydon Aerodrome to Zurich and back in a day, covering the 1,000-mile round trip in 14 hours and using just 54 gallons of petrol.

De Havilland established a worldwide network of sales and service stations for Moths, and conducted a vigorous publicity campaign which included putting a Moth in the window of a store on London's Oxford Street. Dealers provided flying instruction on the aeroplane (one even promised to teach a potential buyer to fly in a single day), while at the company's own airfield at Stag Lane lock-up 'Moth garages' were available at modest weekly rentals, and de Havilland ground staff were on hand to service, wash and prepare your aeroplane for flight on the strength of a telephone call before you motored out to the aerodrome. In the first year of production Moths sold for £885. A year later a 60 hp Moth was priced at £795, and eventually fell to £730 thanks to the economies of

Left: Sir Geoffrey de Havilland.

Below: De Havilland D.H. 60G Gipsy Moth.

large scale production, which had Moths leaving the factory at the rate of two per day at its peak.

The visionary Director of Civil Aviation Sir Sefton Brancker – later to die tragically and needlessly in the crash of the disastrous airship R-101 – ordered 90 Moths for his new government-sponsored flying clubs. It was also 'Branks' who was indirectly responsible for a valuable piece of Moth promotion when he helped a young typist to find backing for a solo flight from England to Australia in 1930. Amy Johnson's

Moth *Jason* (named after the family fish business in Yorkshire) completed the 10,000-mile journey in ten weeks, and is the best-known of all Moths, preserved today in London's Science Museum.

The breathless pace of Moth production soon depleted available stocks of surplus Airdisco-Renault engines from which to create the little Cirrus. Frank Halford was commissioned to design an entirely new engine for the Moth in the autumn of 1926 and by the following summer the classic de Havilland Gipsy engine was born. The combination of the Gipsy, de-rated from its maximum 135 hp to 85 hp in production form, and the Moth airframe created an enduring classic – the D.H.60G Gipsy Moth, which appeared in mid-1928 and swiftly gained publicity by winning the coveted King's Cup air race at 105 mph. Captain de Havilland later took his own Gipsy Moth to a record altitude of 19,980 feet, and test pilot Hubert Broad stayed aloft over Stag Lane for 24

Top left: D.H. Moth trade mark.
Far left: Blue sky, green fields. A Moth in its element. This one is a Gipsy Moth, restored in the colour scheme applied to Amy Johnson's famous *Jason*. Below: Gipsy Moths getting airborne. Both of these aircraft were recovered from Switzerland and restored to better-than-new condition by British antique aeroplane enthusiasts.

Far left: D.H. 82A Tiger Moth with wing-walker performing a Barnstormer act.

Top left: Rear cockpit of a Gipsy Moth. Note the Gosport Tube below cockpit coaming.

Below: Classic take-off attitude displayed by a Tiger Moth.

Bottom: The unique D.H. 51 *Miss Kenya* owned by the Shuttleworth Trust was a larger forerunner of the Moth series, built in 1925.

Below: This D.H. 60M Metal Moth is a rare American-built example, differing from British-built Gipsy Moths in having a welded steel tube fuselage.

Left: The two-seat cabin D.H.87 Hornet Moth first flew in 1934 as a Gipsy Moth replacement.

Cockpit access was improved in the D.H.82A Tiger Moth by moving the cabane struts clear of the front cockpit and sweeping the wing panels back. Compare with Gipsy Moth whose front cockpit was difficult to enter and leave with full flying kit. The long exhaust pipe is an efficient cockpit heater.

hours in a Gipsy Moth fitted with extra fuel tanks. The Gipsy engine was a masterpiece, light, powerful and utterly reliable. To prove its dependability an engine was selected at random from the production line, installed in a company-owned Moth, sealed by official observers, and flown by de Havilland Reserve School flying instructors for 600 hours without maintenance save for routine greasing and oil replenishment. In nine months of day-in, day-out operation the Gipsy flew the equivalent of 51,000 miles. The cost of its eventual overhaul? A little over £7 for replacement parts.

Remarkably, the Gipsy Moth sold for less than its predecessors – £650, including a tool kit, covers for the engine, propeller and cockpits and a choice of colour scheme. A de luxe model came

complete with a set of wheel chocks, a tailskid dolly and a shooting stick. The accommodation, noted a contemporary issue of *Flight* magazine, displayed 'a more artistic lay-out, with instrument board finished in dull cellulose finish, a small pocket above the dashboard for the stowage of gloves, pipes, maps and even – yes, why not? – powder puffs.'

Maintenance, promised the de Havilland sales brochures, was so easy that anyone who could work on a motor car could take care of the Moth's modest needs, and the Gipsy engine could run on ordinary commercial grades of petrol. The sight of a Moth filling up at a roadside garage was not uncommon, and fortunately for present-day Moth owners faced with ever-rising prices of aviation fuel, the motor-fuel approval for the

Gipsy engine still holds good.

To fly in a Moth is to travel back in time to the genteel days of the pre-war flying club, when runways were of grass and always into wind, and there was always someone interesting to talk with while taking tea on the trim lawns outside the clubhouse, watching the aeroplanes – mostly Moths – come and go. At length a pilot would stroll to a Moth, unfurl its wings from their folded position alongside the fuselage and the machine would emerge from slumber like its namesake from a chrysalis. The front seat passenger would have to negotiate the cat's cradle of struts and wires to get aboard, and on the Gipsy had to remember not to trail a hand lazily over the left side of the cockpit, or the long pipe which carried the Gipsy engine's exhaust note would give its own blistering reminder of its presence. In com-

pensation for this small inconvenience the pipe served as an excellent cockpit heater, and the upright cylinders of the Gipsy would also waft back warm air to make the open cockpits cosy.

The reliable Gipsy engine started on the first swing, and with no brakes was off, with a mechanic helping to turn it into wind. Up came the tail as the throttle was opened and she'd be off in a trice, after a run of perhaps 100 yards. Left to itself a Gipsy Moth would take-off unbidden, as the adventurer Sir Francis Chichester once discovered when flying from Croydon in his famous Gipsy Moth *Mme. Elijah*. Chichester thought the instructor with him was flying; the instructor thought Chichester was doing the take off: *Mme. Elijah* just got on with it herself!

Cruising unhurried at 80 mph in calm air the Gipsy was a delight, if anything perhaps a trifle

American-built D.H.60M Metal Moth.

too stable laterally, for the ailerons were heavy and none too effective thanks to differential gearing devised by designer Arthur Hagg which limited the movement of the down-going aileron to reduce adverse yaw in a turn. For slow flight the Handley Page autoslots on the top wing would creep out like nervous mice as the angle of attack increased and airspeed bled off, but it was easy to watch the airspeed when approaching to land or manoeuvring close to the ground thanks to the indicator mounted on the port interplane strut – a calibrated quadrant over which a spring-loaded pointer was moved by the pressure of air moving past the aeroplane. Simple, but effective and surprisingly accurate.

As for landing, it was said that it 'could not be easier', and to prove it Geoffrey de Havilland used to demonstrate power-off approaches with his Moth's throttle fully-closed and the control column held right back in his stomach while the biplane floated safely down, just above the stall to a perfect three-point landing. Unfortunately the day on which his Moth's undercarriage chose to give way was also the day on which a photographer happened to be recording the event!

I doubt that there is any part of the world on which the shadow of some Moth's wings has not fallen, although de Havilland's idea of a people's aeroplane never did come to fruition. Cheap though it was a new Moth cost four or five times the price of a family car, and few people in the 1920s could afford *those*. But I would certainly defend the Moth as the most successful, influential and universally applauded British light aircraft in history. If not an aeroplane for all, then definitely an aeroplane for all time.

FAST AND FURIOUS

There has probably never been a better time to be a pilot in the Royal Air Force than during the 1930s. The grass airfields, silver-doped biplanes with bright-polished engine cowlings gleaming in the summer sun, colourful squadron markings snaking along their flanks and across their wings all helped make the RAF the world's best aero club. It was then, as now, the dream of every young recruit to fly fighters, and the fighter which most of them wanted to fly was the Hawker Fury, a small, light, fast biplane whose open-exhausted supercharged Rolls-Royce Kestrel IIS engine made it the aerial equivalent

Above: The Hawker Tomtit was an unsuccessful contender for a Royal Air Force trainer contract. The sole remaining example is owned by the Shuttleworth Trust at Old Warden.

of a Blower Bentley.

The Fury epitomised the single-seat fighter of the 1930s: nimble, sleek, 30 mph faster than its RAF contemporaries with a maximum speed at altitude of 207 mph. It began life as the Hawker Hornet, a product of the design talent of Sydney Camm, and created a great stir when it first appeared at the 1929 Olympia Aero Show. Trials against the rival Fairey Firefly Mk.IIM saw the Hornet emerge the victor in a competition for the RAF's new interceptor. But the name would not do. According to Air Ministry dictum land-based fighters had to have names beginning with the letter F (and fleet fighters with the letter N). Thus the name Fury was selected and an order was placed in August 1930 for an initial batch of 20 aircraft. The first production Fury made its maiden flight at Brooklands Aerodrome on 25 March 1931 in the hands of test pilot 'Gerry' Sayer. Two months later the first Furies were delivered to 43 Squadron at RAF Tangmere in Sussex to replace their elderly Armstrong Whitworth Siskins.

The Fury set new standards. It was the first RAF interceptor capable of exceeding 200 mph in level flight, and it could climb to 10,000 feet in a little over four minutes. Structurally it was practical, straightforward, employing the classic metal girder construction of square tubes and flat plate fittings which had become a Camm hallmark and was used on all of his internationally successful single- and two-seat biplanes throughout the 1930s – and even on the Hurricane monoplane which was the ultimate Fury development.

Polished cowlings, open exhausts: the Hawker Fury 1, every 1930s schoolboy's dream of a fighter.

The British public had their first chance to see the exciting new fighter at the Hendon Air Display of 1931 when a trio of 43 Squadron pilots performed a faultless aerobatic routine. Its great speed range and the instant throttle response of the 525 hp Kestrel engine made the Fury a fine formation display aircraft, and RAF squadrons – only six of which were ever equipped with the aircraft – took advantage of this. Sixteen-plane tied-together formations were a favourite sight at the Hendon displays, as were the tight diamond formation aerobatics of 1 Squadron's aerobatic team, who did much to boost Britain's image abroad with a polished display at the 1937 Zurich International Air Meeting. Three pilots from 25 Squadron based at RAF Hawkinge in Kent are credited with performing the first-ever formation slow roll in their Furies; even on surviving film it is an impressive manoeuvre, though the pilot in the number two slot never did get his aeroplane quite straightened out in the roll. The Fury was the kind of machine which encouraged aerobatics. It took a strong will *not* to succumb to the desire to loop or roll it.

The Fury's armament comprised a pair of 0.303 Vickers machine-guns mounted in the nose top decking, firing between the revolving propeller blades (not *through* them as is so often quoted) by means of the reliable old First World War vintage Constantinesco interrupter gear. Two thumb triggers on the aircraft's control column activated the guns, which no RAF Fury ever used in anger. The armament provided pilots of 25 Squadron (and others, no doubt) with a ready means of playing a terrible trick on neophyte

Fury pilots. Above the breeches of the two Vickers guns were a pair of flaps which had to be raised when it was necessary to change the locks, and one pilot from 25 discovered that by lowering the Fury's adjustable pilot's seat to the very bottom of its travel and opening these flaps it was possible to fly the aeroplane accurately with your head below the rim of the cockpit. The procedure, then, was this: a new pilot would be flying along, minding his own business when alongside would draw another Fury. He would look across to give his colleague a wave and, to his horror, see an apparently pilotless aeroplane formating on him. After a panic-stricken peel-off and return to base the startled lad would stagger white-faced and shaken into the officers' mess demanding a large medicinal scotch, and down it in a gulp. On enquiring what ailed him the unsuspecting pilot officer, fearful of being thought to lack moral fibre, would confide grudgingly that he had just flown alongside an *empty* Hawker Fury. Whereupon a surly senior officer would disdainfully inform the frightened young man that this Phantom Fury was flown by the spirit of a departed pilot and that it was a matter which should never again be referred to in the officers' mess! Fortunately the sheer sensual delight of flying the Fury would more than compensate for such cruel jokes.

Below: Hawker Hind restored in the colours of the Afghan Air Force by the Shuttleworth Trust.

Right: Sydney Camm's Hawker Hart was an adaptable two-seater used in light bomber and many other roles. This Hart Trainer is preserved in the Royal Air Force Museum at Hendon.

The ultimate Fury development (and yet another contender for the title of the world's most beautiful biplane) was a private venture developed by Hawker in 1933 as an engine test-bed, and known according to taste as the Super Fury or, more commonly, as the High Speed Fury. Initially the High Speed Fury was powered by a 525 hp Rolls-Royce Kestrel IIS engine and was distinguished by its elegant tapered wings and 'V' interplane struts in place of the parallel chord surfaces and 'N' struts of production Furies. Three years of test flying ensued in this guise, powered variously with Kestrel engines of 525 and 600 hp, and by 695 hp Goshawk engines with evaporative cooling, for which leading edge condensers were fitted to the upper wing, restoring the familiar Fury shape (and, to my mind at least, destroying much of the High Speed Fury's undeniable beauty). The sole High Speed Fury was claimed to have reached a maximum speed of 261 mph while on trials at the Royal Aircraft Establishment at Martlesham Heath. Fast, but not fast enough to ensure the survival of the biplane as an interceptor, though the High Speed Fury did pave the way for Hawker's monoplane fighter, the Hurricane.

The ultimate development of the Fury biplane was the High Speed Fury. Note tapered lower wing, condensers set into upper wing leading edge for evaporative cooling trials.

Sydney Camm.

ASK ANY PILOT

The big red and white biplane comes thundering along the runway billowing white smoke like a locomotive, holding low while the airspeed builds up and its chromed bracing wires start to sing, then rears up as if mortally stricken, gyrating insanely, and continues on its way leaving a perfect knot of smoke tied in the sky. The pilot: Bob Lyjak, a Polish-American professor of mathematics at the University of Michigan and veteran airshow performer. The manoeuvre: Lyjak's own invention, which he calls the *Cobra Roll* after the motion of the snake's lethal strike. The biplane: a favourite at airshows for half a century – the Waco Taperwing. It is pronounced

Above: American airshow performer Bob Lyjak flies this Waco Taperwing with one of the most effective smoke systems in the business.

Right: Wright Whirlwind-engined Waco CTO Taperwing.

Wah-co, never whacko or way-co, and it is an acronym for the Weaver Aircraft Company.

Paradoxically, George E. 'Buck' Weaver, whose name the company bore, played little part in the Waco story. It happened that in 1919 two life-long friends from Michigan, Clayton John Brukner and James Elwood 'Sam' Junkin stopped in the town of Lorain, Ohio, and there met Weaver and his barnstorming partner Charlie Meyers. Weaver had a damaged Canuck biplane, and Sam and Clayt wanted to get into the aircraft building and repair business, so a partnership was struck, and since Buck Weaver was well-known locally and would likely be able to raise some finance in the town, his name was used for the company title.

Plans were laid for a passenger-carrying biplane, using a stock of surplus Curtiss Jenny parts and 90 hp OX-5 engines which Brukner and Junkin bought for $350 the lot, wings for as little as $4 apiece, a dozen propellers for $36. The three-passenger biplane was called the Waco Four (they had built three small aeroplanes before meeting Weaver) and it was used to barnstorm in the Lorain area with Clayt Brukner acting as wing-walker to attract paying passengers. In 1920 both Weaver and Charlie Meyers went their own ways, and the following summer the company moved to Medina, Ohio where three Waco Fives were built and sold. Another move took Brukner and Junkin to the town of Troy, where a young man named Alden Sampson II agreed to buy $20,000 worth of stock in their enterprise which was renamed the Advance Aircraft Company, though the Waco

Centre left: Few would argue that the Taperwing design was aesthetically near perfect.

Top left: Typical of the Waco cabin biplanes, a YKS-7.

Bob Lyjak at work in the 'unbreakable' Taperwing.

name was retained for all of their aircraft.

Advance built three more designs by 1924 (in which year Buck Weaver died from blood poisoning) and in 1925 introduced the classic Waco Model Nine, 'the new steel Waco' which incorporated a welded steel tube fuselage and, save for the OX-5 engine, was the first Waco not to make use of the bargain-basement stock of surplus Jenny parts. The Waco Nine sold for $2,500 in 1925, reduced to $2,250 the following year, and was soon outselling its rivals four-to-one. Among early customers was Ball Airlines, later to become Pennsylvania-Central, and now United Airlines. The Waco Nine was a sturdy, dependable machine. When the US Air Commerce Regulations were introduced in 1926 requiring all aircraft manufacturers to have their aeroplanes certificated to minimum standards a Waco Nine was tested to destruction by the US Army at McCook Field and found to be able to withstand a 7.5g load; the required certification standard was only 6g.

From the Nine evolved the 1927 Waco Ten, which had four ailerons instead of the Nine's two and featured the first hydraulic shock-absorbing landing gear on a light aeroplane. *Quicker take-off, faster climb, higher top speed* promised Advance's advertisements, 'New fans, let your air-wise friend explain the student value and student safety of Waco Ten features and Waco's unrivalled performance. He knows the advantages of an all-altitude airplane of proven superior performance. Ask him.' The three-seat Waco Ten (two passengers sat side-by-side in the open front cockpit, a distinctive Waco feature on many open-cockpit models) was offered with an OX-5, OXX-6, Hispano-Suiza or the new Wright Whirlwind engine. Charlie Meyers, now hired by Brukner and Junkin as a test pilot, flew one of the new aircraft to victory in the 1927 Trans-

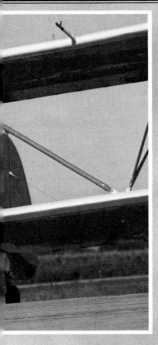

1927 Waco Ten was the aeroplane which established the Waco company. It was offered with OX-5, OXX-6, Hisso and Wright engines, and seated two passengers in the front open cockpit.

Far left: Jim Franklin performing his insanely low inverted ribbon pick-up in a hybrid Waco JMF-7.

Centre left: Diagonal strut bracing was a feature of many cabin Wacos such as this YKS-7.

Left: Faultless restoration work on a Waco CTO Taperwing by American antique aircraft enthusiast John Turgyan.

Right: A clear view of the wing markings on Bob Lyjak's Waco taperwing and left the smoke systems at full power.

continental Air Race between Long Island and Spokane, Washington, his Waco *The Wings of Progress* finishing nearly half an hour ahead of his nearest class rival. It was the first of many Waco racing victories, and in 1928 a Ten won the fourth Commercial Reliability· Tour (promoted by Edsel Ford of the Ford Motor Company). Sales boomed, aided by an efficient network of Waco distributors who easily sold the five aircraft a day coming out of the Troy factory.

A new plant was built to cope with demand, and from here, in 1928, the first Waco Taperwing emerged. 'Taperwing' referred to a new wing de-

sign devised by Advance's engineer Ed Green at the suggestion of Charlie Meyers, a wing of perfect aesthetic planform which was intended to increase the Waco's speed and roll rate. It was offered on the 225 hp Wright J-5 engined Waco Tens and was to become the trademark of one of the world's superlative aerobatic biplanes (standard Waco Tens were thereafter referred to as 'Straightwings').

The first Taperwing was sold to racing pilot Johnny Livingston, who promptly won the 1928 Transcontinental Air Race from New York to Los Angeles in it. At the Los Angeles National Air

Races in September of that year, aerobatic pilot Freddie Lund captivated the crowds with a dazzling display in a Taperwing, was hired by the company to replace Charlie Meyers as test pilot, and met his future wife, Betty, all on the same day. Lund was one of the great Taperwing exponents, flying a beautiful candy-striped red and white 300 hp Wright-engined machine in which he specialised in punishing outside loops. On one such manoeuvre Fearless Freddie, 'The Man Without Nerves', was catapulted from the Taperwing's cockpit when his seat belt gave way. He managed to catch hold of the Waco's upper wing and was able to haul himself back into the cockpit and regain control. He died in a midair collision during an air race in 1931. Betty Lund continued to demonstrate the Taperwing and sponsored the first US aerobatic trophy in her husband's memory. Few indeed were the airshow and aerobatics pilots of the thirties who did not fly Taperwings: Len Povey, personal pilot to the Cuban president Fulgencio Batista took the Freddie Lund Trophy in 1933; Joe Mackey, the 1936 winner; Tex Rankin, 1937 international aerobatic champion; Art Davis, Roger Don Rae, all flew the wonderful, unbreakable (no one ever has pulled one apart) Waco Taperwings, which also sold in great numbers to military governments in South America as pursuit ships or trainers.

The Taperwing was the beginning of a diversity of Waco models, the Advance Aircraft Company having once again changed its name, to Waco Aircraft Company, in June 1929. Waco's motto was: *Ask Any Pilot*. The first thing you should ask any pilot is to explain to you the confusion of aircraft type designations which accompanied the expansion of the model line started by the Taperwing. Waco model numbers were based on a three letter designation initially: the first letter denoted engine type, the second wing design, the third the Waco series number. Thus an ATO was a Wright J-5 engined (A) Taperwing (T) Model 10 (O). As the Waco range expanded a numeral was also added to denote sub-type, and the result was a jumble which I believe takes the skills of a master code-breaker to decipher. To eavesdrop on a conversation between members of the National Waco Club in the United States is a surreal journey through a world of Orwellian newsspeak: 'That a UPF? No, it's an IBA. Bob's here in the YKC and there's a guy back there thinks he's found parts of a JHD or maybe a WHD in South America. I'm still flying my old ZKS-7, and I have an EGC-8 in the shop for rebuilding . . .'.

I will not even try to interpret this, but it is worth observing that the UPF-7 was widely used for the training of fliers under the Civilian Pilot Training programme in the 1940s, and because it was ordered in quantity until 1942, is the most numerous of the surviving Wacos, a three-seater

powered by a 220 hp Continental radial engine which Waco afficionados claim is some 15 mph faster than the similarly-powered PT-17 Stearman, its arch-rival. An airshow pilot named Jim Franklin from San Angelo, Texas has one which he has modified with a *500 hp* Pratt & Whitney engine, three-bladed propeller and a single cockpit moved way back almost to the fin like a Gee Bee racer's. He calls it a JMF-7 (a designation never used so far as I can tell), has it painted an evil black, and uses it to perform a special kind of aerial madness involving picking up a ribbon held at waist level by two assistants while he flies the Waco inverted trailing the pick-up hook from his fin tip. He used to balance the ribbon across a pair of Coca-Cola bottles. To finish his act he taxies the Waco all the way back to his parking spot with the tail cocked high in the air and his smoke system going full blast. Last time I saw him he totally obscured the act which followed his and caused the airshow commentator to reassure the pollution-minded crowd that the Environmental Protection Agency had checked the smoke and found it 100 per cent non-toxic. A good thing to know when you are flying inverted at 120 knots just three feet up. Choking to death would be too ironic!

Aside from the Taperwing, perhaps best loved among the many Waco biplanes were the luxury cabin models produced throughout the 1930s as executive transports or personal aircraft for the rich. Continual refinement of the basic four/five seat cabin design, which included the 1938 N Model with a tricycle undercarriage – one of few biplanes so equipped and the only one save for the Russian M-15 Mielec jet ever to go into production – culminated in the svelte ARE and SRE Airistocrats of 1939, five passenger aircraft which could top 200 mph (in 450 hp Pratt & Whitney Wasp powered SRE form) and were rivals for Walter Beech's Staggerwing. *Ask Any Pilot*? Certainly, any pilot who knows Wacos. But be warned: you may not be able to stop him once he gets started!

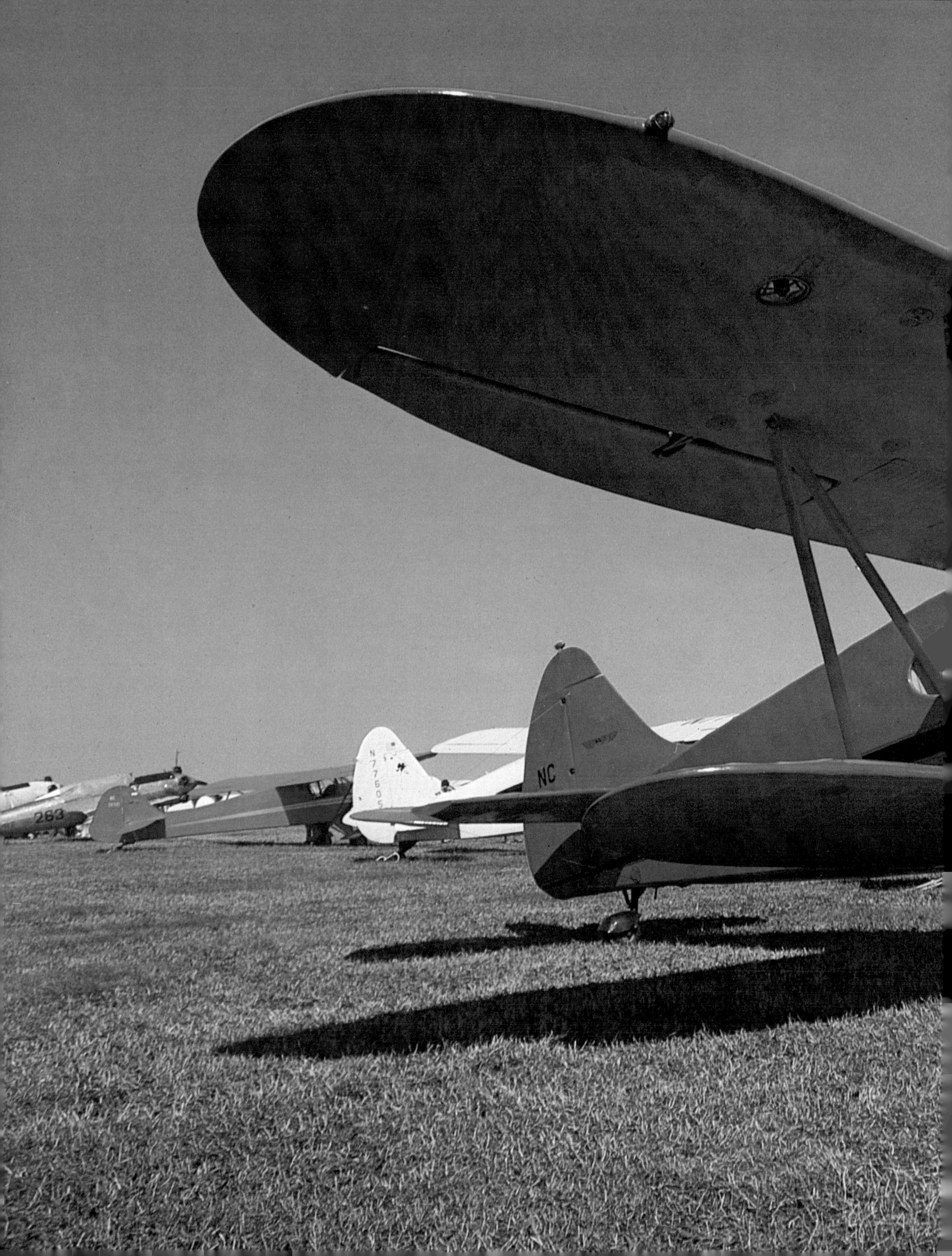
NC
N77605
263

Above: The Waco UPF-7 was a US Army trainer, manufactured in large numbers for the Civilian Pilot Training Programme.

Left: Magnificent Waco YQC-6 pictured at a gathering of the National Waco Club in the United States.

GRUMMAN'S FLYING BARRELS

A name held dear to the hearts of veteran US Navy aviators – *Fifi* – was not, as you might suppose, an exotic dancer in a Pensacola night club, but the first product of a company whose association with the US Navy was to be long, continuing to this day with the F-14 Tomcat. The Grumman Aircraft Engineering Corporation was formed in December 1929 by Leroy Grumman, Leon Swirbul and Bill Schwendler, three former employees of the Loening company who preferred the comforts of Long Island to those of Pennsylvania when Loening moved there in 1928. So they set up shop in a garage in Baldwin, Long Island and began soliciting the US Navy for an order for an amphibious aircraft float, meanwhile building and repairing truck bodies to pay their bills.

In time the navy ordered Grumman floats in quantity, and the three engineers grew bolder, approaching the US Navy Bureau of Aeronautics with a proposal for a radical new two-seat shipboard fighter which they promised would perform better than any existing single-seater then in shipboard service. A contract was awarded, and on 29 December 1931 the prototype Grumman XFF-1 made its first flight, and was ferried that same day to the naval air station at Anacostia to begin its evaluation trials.

The XFF-1 was a radical, not to say controversial machine. It had an all-metal monocoque fuselage, an enclosed cockpit, which gave rise to no little concern among pilots at Anacostia anticipating the need for a rapid exit, and the first retractable undercarriage seen on a navy fighter prototype. The undercarriage, which was drawn up vertically to lay flush with the pot-bellied fuselage sides, was a Loening invention which had been used very successfully on amphibians, but it too gave rise to misgivings among carrier pilots used to the 'slam 'em down' techniques of deck landing.

In the event all the doubters were proved wrong. The XFF-1, powered by a 620 hp Wright Cyclone R-1820-E engine, recorded a maximum speed of 197 mph in trials, ten miles per hour better than the single-seat Boeing F4B-2 then in its first year of naval service, and it was more manoeuvrable. Anacostia's test pilots thought the brakes inadequate but otherwise concluded that the Grumman was a fine aeroplane, and the Bureau of Aeronautics duly ordered 27 production FF-1s (hence *Fifi*), which were powered by 700 hp Wright Cyclones, pushing the maximum level flight speed above 200 mph. *Fifi*'s fighter service with the navy was short-lived, though scouting SF-1s and FF-2 dual control trainers

Previous page: The last of the Grumman Barrels was the Cyclone-engined F3F-2.

Left: 'Fifi', the Grumman FF-1 which was the US Navy's first enclosed cockpit, retractable-undercarriage fighter.

lingered on until 1942.

Even before the FF-1 went operational Leroy Grumman and his partners had anticipated the trend away from two-seat fighters and had begun work on a single-seat successor, the XF2F-1, for which a prototype contract was awarded on 2 November 1932. This aeroplane, shorter than the FF-1, was even more barrel-like, with a corpulent fuselage like a bumble-bee's. The 625 hp Pratt & Whitney Wasp Junior engine was smooth cowled on the prototype, which first flew on 18 October 1933, but so tightly wrapped on production F2F-1s that the cowling had to be bulged to accommodate the rocker covers, giving it a distinctive 'helmeted' appearance. The XF2F-1 was an outstanding performer, having a maximum speed of 229 mph and an initial rate of climb in excess of 3,000 feet per minute, but the short-coupled fuselage made it directionally less stable than the *Fifi*, and prone to spinning if mishandled in slow flight. A four-inch fuselage extension went some way to improving directional stability. The navy decided experienced pilots could live with its spinning characteristics,

and ordered 54 aircraft, the first of which joined VF-2B 'Fighting Two' squadron aboard USS *Lexington* in February 1935. Fighting Two flew their F2F-1s from *Lexington* for five years, until 30 September 1940 when they were relegated to training duties.

While the US Navy had been prepared to tolerate the less than desirable characteristics of the second Grumman fighter, Leroy Grumman was working on further refinements with a major redesign, again begun before the previous model had entered squadron service. The XF3F-1 prototype, funded by the navy to the tune of $76,000, had a 22-inch fuselage stretch to overcome the F2F-1's directional problems, a 3½-foot wingspan extension and a number of aerodynamic refinements. It flew for the first time from Long Island on 20 March 1935, and made three uneventful test flights that day. Two days later Jimmy Collins, a freelance test pilot, took the XF3F-1 up for the mandatory programme of ten terminal velocity dives required by the navy. It was to have been Collins' last day as a test pilot. He intended to take up a career as a writer. As it turned out this was Collins' last day on earth.

After completing nine dives in five flights he took off again late in the day from the airfield at Farmingdale, climbed to 18,000 feet and pushed the Grumman over into a very steep dive. At 8,000 feet the XF3F-1 was seen to nose up and then disintegrate, tumbling into Long Island's Pinelawn Cemetery. Collins was supposed to have demonstrated a 9g recovery from the final dive. The accelerometer in the wrecked biplane's cockpit had recorded a maximum load of between 11-15g during the recovery, and the wings and engine had been torn out of the aeroplane. Collins' death shocked the American public, for he was a well-known and popular figure. He wrote regular columns for the New York *Daily News* and *Saturday Evening Post*, and had at one time penned his own obituary lest his death should cause him to miss his editor's deadline. Entitled *I Am Dead* it contained this chillingly prescient line: 'The cold but vibrant fuselage was the last thing to feel my warm and living flesh.'

To a less well respected company the loss of a new prototype so early in its trials and in such spectacular fashion might have killed off the whole project, but the navy bureau ordered a

named Buffalo) monoplane fighter proved the biplane traditionalists right and turned out to be a failure. Grumman duly drew up plans for the new biplane, but also worked on a parallel project for a monoplane, and reported back to the navy that a more powerful engine on the F3F-1 would provide performance equal to that of the projected XF4F-1. The Bureau of Aeronautics concurred: Grumman would build 81 F3F-2s (the largest single order yet received) with 1,000 hp Wright R-1820-22 Cyclone engines (maximum continuous horsepower was 850), and the XF4F project would be developed as a monoplane, later to become the legendary F4F Wildcat.

The F3F-2 was the final refinement of the Grumman barrel, with a maximum speed of 264 mph. One additional aircraft was custom built to the order of Major Alford Williams, a former navy test pilot and aviation manager of the Gulf Oil Company, who was also a noted aviation writer under the *nom de plume* 'Tattered Wing Tips'. Al Williams' aircraft was a hybrid combination of the Cyclone-engined F3F-2's fuselage with the shorter wings of the F2F-1. It was designated Grumman G-22 and named *Gulfhawk II*, resplendent in a high gloss orange, white and blue sunburst paint scheme with polished struts

second XF3F-1 which flew two months later. It too crashed, on the day of its delivery to Anacostia when pilot Lee Gehlbach was demonstrating a ten-turn spin. The spin went flat and Gehlbach bailed out. He reported that like its predecessor the XF3F-1 was directionally unstable, so the third prototype incorporated a small ventral fin to increase the vertical stabiliser area, and this aeroplane completed its trials without further incident, although the navy temporarily reduced their maximum g loading requirement from 9g to 7.5g, forbade intentional spinning in all new naval aircraft until they had been tested in the new NACA spin research wind-tunnel at Langley Field, and cautioned squadron pilots of the low stick forces on the production F3F-1 which could easily lead to overstressing and structural failure if a pilot pulled too hard when recovering from a dive.

First deliveries of the F3F-1, which was powered by a 700 hp (take-off rating) Pratt & Whitney R-1535-84 Twin Wasp, began in January 1936. Though it was bigger and heavier, the refined F3F-1 had the same maximum speed as the F2F-1, though its climb rate was inferior. Armament, which was never used in combat, comprised a .303 Browning machine-gun, and a .50 Browning in the upper forward fuselage.

A fourth Grumman navy biplane was ordered on 6 March 1936, the XF4F-1 which was to be powered by the then experimental Wright XR-1670 engine, and was seen by navy staff as a back-up in case the Brewster XF2A-1 (later

Far left: Major Al Williams, Gulf Oil's flamboyant aviation manager, pictured in the cockpit of his Grumman G-22 *Gulfhawk II*.

Below: Al Williams 'on top' in *Gulfhawk II*.

Left: More Flying Boot than Barrel is this Grumman J2F-6 Duck amphibian.

and bracing wires. Williams installed an inverted fuel and oil system which permitted up to 30 minutes' inverted flight and used the immaculate *Gulfhawk II* from 1936 until 1948 for airshow performances and for research work, testing Gulf fuels, oils and lubricants. In 1938 *Gulfhawk II* was shipped to Europe for a tour of Britain, France, Holland and Germany, where the German First World War ace Ernst Udet became the only man other than Williams ever to fly it, in exchange for a flight by Williams in the new Messerschmitt Bf 109 fighter. On 11 October 1948 Williams flew the Grumman to Washington D.C.'s National Airport, performed one last aerobatic routine, then removed *Gulfhawk II*'s control column and handed the aircraft over to the Smithsonian Institution. It is displayed today in the National Air & Space Museum. Two other civilian F3Fs were built as two-seaters, one of which also went to Williams as *Gulfhawk III*.

Leroy Grumman's flying barrels were the American biplane's last great stand against the inevitable onslaught of the monoplane in naval, and indeed most other, fields of aviation. They were innovative, introducing retractable undercarriages to shipboard fighter aircraft for the first time (incidentally, that knock-kneed undercarriage was hand cranked, up to 32 turns depending on the model – you could always tell a new pilot by the way the Grumman wobbled after take-off as he tried to fly with one hand and crank the handle with the other), and established Grumman as builders of reliable aeroplanes.

GLORIOUS GLOSTER

The last of the great Royal Air Force biplane fighters signalled the end of an era and an end to peace. H. P. 'Harry' Folland, whose association with RAF fighters began in 1914, designed the Gloster Gladiator, then known uninspiringly as the Gloster S.S.37, to the famous Air Ministry specification F.7/30 which was to lead at length to the Supermarine Spitfire and Hawker Hurricane monoplane fighters. The S.S.37 was a private venture submitted to the Air Ministry late in the day, the prototype flying in the hands of Gerry Sayer on 12 September 1934.

The S.S.37 was a refined successor to the Gloster Gauntlet which was even then not in squadron service with the RAF. Fuselage and tail unit were almost identical, but Folland adopted single-bay wings for the new machine, doubled the Gauntlet's armament by adding a Lewis gun under each wing to the two fuselage-mounted Vickers, and incorporated a cantilever undercarriage unit fitted with Sir George Dowty's internally-sprung wheels. The engine was a 645 hp Bristol Mercury VIS.2.

Ministerial resistance to the monoplane and the too-radical features of several of the other biplane contenders for F.7/30 brought Glosters a contract in July 1935 for 23 production aircraft, with a further 180 ordered two months later. Production Gladiators differed markedly from the S.S.37. The Mercury IX of 840 hp was substituted for the earlier powerplant, a sliding cockpit

canopy was installed which was operated by a bicycle chain and ratchet arrangement, hydraulically-operated flaps fitted to all four wing panels – which was and is rare in biplanes – a standard six instrument blind flying panel provided for the first time on a RAF fighter, and the provisional Vickers/Lewis armament replaced with four Browning machine-guns on all aircraft after the first 70 had been delivered, two synchronised to fire between the revolving propeller blades, the other pair installed in blister fairings beneath the lower wings. With a two-blade wooden Watts propeller the Gladiator's top speed was 248 mph. Its rate of climb, 2,300 feet per minute, was much the same as the Gauntlet's, but it was a better handling machine, some say second only to the Hawker Fury, though forward visibility between the cabane struts was poor and despite the enclosed canopy the lack of any cockpit heating made high altitude flying a misery.

When the first Gladiators entered service with 72 Squadron at RAF Tangmere, Sussex in February 1937 they were already outdated stopgaps awaiting the inevitable rise of the monoplane fighter. Nine other squadrons were equipped during the year out of 25 eventually to receive the Gladiator. By the outbreak of war the biplane had largely been superseded in Fighter Command, although 13 RAF squadrons still had them and speculation ran high in the messes as to how the anachronistic Gladiator would fare against the Luftwaffe's Messerschmitt Bf 109s. Ironically Gladiators were the first RAF aircraft to intercept a Luftwaffe raid on Britain when they attacked German bombers over the Firth of

Forth in September 1939. On 17 October three pilots from D Flight, 607 Squadron forced down a Dornier Do.18 flying-boat off the coast of Northumberland, and Gladiator-equipped 247 Squadron based at Plymouth-Roborough was active in the Battle of Britain defending the naval dockyard at Devonport.

But it was overseas that the Gladiator saw most action, in France, Egypt, Syria and Greece. Two wartime actions are synonymous with the last RAF biplane fighter. In April 1940 263 Squadron were embarked aboard the aircraft carrier HMS *Glorious* at Scapa Flow for Norway where they were to oppose the German invasion forces. They flew off the carrier which was in Norwegian waters and arrived at a frozen lake near Lesjaskog on 24 April, planning to use the lake surface as a makeshift airfield. Overhead German bomber crews watched with fascination,

Below, right, previous page and over page: Differing views of the Shuttleworth Trust's Gloster Gladiator displayed by a Squadron Leader "Dicky" Martin at Old Warden.

and returned at dawn next day to bomb the lake's icy surface, which was melting anyway. All but four of the Gladiators sank. A month later HMS *Glorious* returned with another 18 Gladiators, this time operating from a proper grass airfield near Barduföss in the Arctic. 263 Squadron's pilots, who had destroyed six Luftwaffe aircraft in that first aborted action, destroyed a further 26 in two weeks of brave fighting. Pilot Officer Jacobsen of 263 took on six Heinkel He IIIs and two Junkers JU-88s alone on 2 June 1940. By out-manoeuvring the bomber he forced one Junkers to fly into the side of a fjord and shot down three of the He IIIs. Five days later 263's Gladiators were once again shipped home, but the ten surviving aircraft and most of the pilots were lost when *Glorious* was attacked by the battleships *Scharnhorst* and *Gneisenau* and sunk on the way to Scotland. Six pilots, embarked on another ship, arrived safely.

Two weeks later Italy (which also had some biplane fighters still in front-line service) entered the war, and briefly the defence of the Mediterranean island of Malta rested on a handful of Sea Gladiators (the Sea Gladiator had a three-blade Fairey-Reed propeller, A-frame

arrester hook, catapult points and a survival dinghy carried beneath its belly in a pod, and had been HMS *Glorious'* fighter defence while she was ferrying the RAF Gladiators to Norway) borrowed from the Fleet Air Arm by RAF pilots. Four biplanes fought a brave battle against the *Regia Aeronautica*'s bomber forces between 11 and 28 June 1940, though they could do little but attempt to scatter the Italian formations and distract their bomb aimers. Appropriately the Maltese dubbed three of the four Sea Gladiators *Faith, Hope* and (less appositely) *Charity*, though contrary to the perpetuated myth, the aircraft never carried their names.

The action off Malta effectively ended the Gladiator's service. The significance of this aeroplane – the 'Glad' – is that it was a tough and sweet-flying machine, outmoded from the start, but the last (and some might argue the best) of a romantic breed: the biplane fighter.

AGELESS CHAMPION

His name was Constantin Cantacuzene. Prince Constantin Cantacuzene, though he liked his friends to call him 'Buzz', and if you chanced to witness one of his occasional forays into the airshow world during the 1950s you would probably have called him mad. Cantacuzene was an aristocrat, a member of the Romanian royal family who shot down 60 Russian aircraft during the Second World War and later fled Romania's communist regime in a DC-2 airliner (allegedly cutting down a line of cavalry who were trying to prevent his escape) to live in exile in Spain. He admired beautiful women, had a penchant for English fish and chips, and had the craziest line in airshow finales. He would come gliding in at the end of his routine in his little silver biplane giving every appearance of having finished his display, then just as the wheels brushed the grass he would gun the throttle and do a snap-roll right off the deck, close the throttle again and finish his landing before the astonished crowd could even bring their hands to their mouths. There are few aeroplanes in which such liberties may be taken – more than once at least – and Buzz's biplane was one of the best – a Bücker Bu 133 Jungmeister.

Carl Clemens Bücker had flown with the Imperial German Navy Air Service in the First World War before moving to Sweden, where he ran Svenska Aero AB before returning to Germany in 1932, where he founded his own aircraft company Bücker-Flugzeugbau GmbH at Berlin's Johannisthal Airport. At this time the *National-Sozialistiche Deutsche Arbeiter Partei* was in the ascendant and Adolf Hitler's Secretary of State for Air, Erhard Milch, was making no secret of the Nazis' plan to rebuild German air strength which had been crippled

Count Otto von Hagenburg practising for the 1936 Olympics in his Jungmeister.

under the terms of the Treaty of Versailles. His first priority was training aeroplanes.

Bücker had brought with him from Sweden a brilliant young engineer named Anders J. Andersson. Within six months their first aeroplane was ready, the Bücker Bü 131 Jungmann (Young Man), which flew on 27 April 1934. The Jungmann was a masterly piece of engineering: extraordinarily light, with a welded tube fuselage in which the maximum diameter of the tubular members was just three quarters of an inch and the diameter was progressively reduced between the root of the lower wing and tail surfaces no less than five times. Each wing panel, bare, weighed only 25 pounds, yet the biplane was tremendously strong and performed with indecent agility on an 80 hp Hirth HM60R four cylinder inline engine. The two-seat Jungmann was soon in such demand for the *Deutscher Luftsport Verband*, the German sport-flying organisation which was a barely disguised training school for the embryonic Luftwaffe, that Bücker was forced to find bigger premises, and in 1935 he moved to another Berlin airfield, Rangsdorf. Here it was that Andersson began work on a second biplane design. While it was excellent as a trainer the Jungmann lacked power for advanced aerobatics. Andersson had in mind a 'Super

Jungmann', which would be a single-seater powered by engines in the 135-160 hp range, and to appease the military purse holders it was pointed out that such an aeroplane would help develop the flying skills of Germany's future fighter pilots.

Andersson's dedication to weight reduction reached its peak in the new Jungmeister (Young Champion) which weighed a paltry 937 pounds empty. About 75 per cent of the Jungmann's components had been adapted for the new aircraft, which had shorter wings and fuselage. In prototype form the Jungmeister was powered by a 135 hp Hirth HM6 inline engine, but production versions had 160 hp Siemens-Halske SH-14A seven cylinder radials.

The Jungmeister's appearance in 1936 was timely, for it was the year of the XIth Olympiad, and Germany was the host nation. For the first (and to date only) time aerobatics was included as an Olympic event, and the Jungmeister lived up to its name in the flying competitions held at Berlin's Tempelhof Aerodrome with Count Otto von Hagenburg taking the champion's title. Von Hagenburg's speciality, first seen at the Olympic Games, was an eye-level inverted pass, his Jungmeister's fin tip barely more than two or three feet from the ground. He won the World Cup for

The two seat Bücker Jungmann, first flown in April 1934, was an extraordinary piece of engineering.

Left: Alex Papana's chequered Jungmeister was taken to the United States aboard the airship *Hindenburg*.

Below: The prototype Jungmeister had a Hirth inline engine. Production aircraft had 160 hp Siemens-Halske radials with 'helmeted' cowls.

Bottom: Airline pilot Alex Papana was a noted pre-war aerobatic pilot who exploited the Jungmeister's snap-rolling agility.

international aerobatics at Zurich the following year, against a field which included nine Jungmeisters among 13 contestants, and two months later was invited to perform at the National Air Races at Cleveland, Ohio.

On this occasion von Hagenburg got just a little *too* low. The Jungmeister's fin ploughed in and he made a fearsome-looking inverted landing from which he walked away, to continue his act in another Bücker borrowed from Romanian pilot Alex Papana whose Jungmeister had been brought to the United States in 1936 in the hold of the airship *Hindenburg*. He specialised in hesitation rolls, snap rolls and picking up a handkerchief with a hook on his Bücker's wingtip, and surprised the American aerobatics world in 1937 by placing second in the International Aerobatic Championships at St. Louis, his first entry in a US contest. Papana's Jungmeister never returned to Europe. It was sold to the great American aerobatic flier Mike Murphy, who was never beaten while flying it, and was later acquired by the legendary Bevo Howard from Charleston, North Carolina, who flew it in airshows and competitions for nearly three decades.

He died in it when the Bücker struck a tree during an inverted pass at an airshow. Rumours had it that Bevo had died at the controls, or that he had been paralysed by the bite of a black widow spider found in the wrecked aeroplane. The accident investigators were more prosaic: they concluded that Bevo had uncharacteristically failed to refuel the Jungmeister before his display and that he had run out of fuel and hit the unseen tree (the only one in the area, ironically) while attempting to roll the biplane erect for a forced landing. Fortunately his Bücker was salvaged, and now hangs (upside down, naturally) in the National Air & Space Museum in Washington D.C.

Anders Andersson's superb design remained the ultimate aerobatic machine for 20 years. It was also built in Switzerland, by Dornier-Werke at Altenrhein, and by CASA in Spain, whence came another of its great virtuosos, Count José Aresti (aerobatics, and Jungmeisters particularly, seem to hold a special fascination for European nobility). Aresti invented the *Sistema Aerocriptografico Aresti*, a shorthand method of writing aerobatic manoeuvres in graphic symbol

form, and as fate would have it, he played a major part in eclipsing the Bücker in international unlimited aerobatic competition. Aresti awarded a difficulty or 'K' factor to each manoeuvre, and since he flew a Jungmeister he awarded low marks to those figures which he found easy in his aeroplane and progressively higher marks for those which the Bücker would do less willingly. Thus the highest points were assigned to manoeuvres in the vertical plane, when the aircraft is yo-yoing up and down the sky, and this paved the way for the Czechoslovakian Zlin monoplanes to succeed the Bücker as the foremost aerobatic aircraft.

But there are still many pilots who would argue that for sheer handling pleasure the Jungmeister is unmatched. Its control harmony is very nearly perfect, the surfaces statically and aerodynamically balanced, nestled in roller bearings for fingertip response whatever the airspeed, effective, light and precise so that any manoeuvre, especially in the rolling plane at which the Bücker excels, may be started or stopped with awesome exactness. Which is why old 'Buzz' Cantacuzene died in his bed.

Left: Distinctive features of the Jungmeister are the forward-raked undercarriage legs and 'helmeted' engine cowling. Below: Although it is British-owned this Jungmeister carries the colours of the Deutscher Luftsport Verband – the pre-war German sport flying organisation.

TIGER TIGER

I wish that I could tell you that the de Havilland D.H.82 Tiger Moth, beloved (or accursed) mentor of countless hundreds of thousands of pilots, was a product of inspired genius, or at the very least, of meticulous planning, but it was not so. The truth is that the Tiger was a classic example of eyeball engineering, cobbled together piecemeal, an engine from here, an airframe from there, trial, error and a touch of good fortune.

The international acceptance of the D.H.60 Moths inspired de Havillands to offer the aeroplane as a trainer for the Royal Air Force in 1931, but the Air Ministry was not happy with the Gipsy Moth design which placed the centre-section fuel tank directly above the front cockpit, making rapid exit in an emergency all but impossible for a flying instructor encumbered with full military flying kit. The obvious solution was to move the offending centre section forwards until the cabane struts were completely clear of the front cockpit. That put the aircraft's centre of gravity behind the centre of pressure, so de Havilland's chief designer Arthur Hagg swept the wings back by the simple expedient of shortening each rear spar. In September 1931 a prototype, powered by a 120 hp Gipsy III inverted inline engine from the new Puss Moth monoplane, was despatched for trials at the Aircraft and Armament Experimental Establishment at Martlesham Heath, where it was received with cautious enthusiasm. A production prototype D.H.82 was ordered and was flying within a month. The Air Ministry chose the name Tiger Moth ('somewhat unwisely in our opinion,' noted *Flight*, pointing out that the name had already been used for the

D.H.71 racing monoplane of 1927). The Ministry had had little choice. Elementary trainers had to have names beginning with the letter T and nature had failed to provide any other suitably prefixed member of the moth family! *Flight*'s fears of confusion were unfounded in any case. Within a very few years Tiger Moth became synonymous with the training biplane and the little racer was forgotten.

Thirty-five Tiger Moth Mark Is were ordered for the Royal Air Force initially, and in all 134 were built, including 20 manufactured in Norway and Sweden. The improved, archetypal D.H.82A was introduced in 1934 with a 130 hp Gipsy Major 1 engine and plywood rear fuselage decking in place of the stringers and fabric of the earlier model. It was this Tiger Moth, the RAF's Mark II, which was the major production model, built on lines at the de Havilland factory at Hatfield, at the Morris Motor Works at Cowley, Oxfordshire and in Australia, Canada, New Zealand, Norway, Portugal and Sweden. The exact number of Tigers built is a matter of constant dispute among those who make it their business to study such matters. I take no side in the argument save to say that the most often quoted figure is 9,231. The Canadian D.H.82Cs differed from their British counterparts in a number of ways, mostly in deference to the harsh environment in which they were operated. The most obvious difference was a cockpit canopy, to repel the icy darts which penetrate your body from every direction in an open-cockpit Tiger, making a good flying jacket essential even on balmy summer days.

Trickier to fly than the contemporary Avro Tutor, tetchy with those whose handling was sloppy, and having an irritating knack of magnifying any shortcoming in piloting tech-

A Tiger Moth flies over the field at Crux Easton, near Newbury, which Geoffrey de Havilland used as his personal airstrip at the family home in Berkshire.

nique, the Tiger Moth made a fine training aeroplane, popular with instructors (except for its Gosport tube inter-cockpit communication system, whose black rubber mouthpiece left its mark on them at the end of a long day's flying), and the bane of trainees' lives. It was said with some justification that if you could fly a Tiger Moth you could fly *anything* – those hundreds of thousands who mastered the machine really had learned to fly!

Not that it was all hard work. There is one famous tale told about pupils of No. 18 Elementary Flying Training School stationed at Fairoaks Aerodrome in Surrey during the war. The nearby Vickers aircraft factory at Weybridge was heavily ringed with barrage balloon defences, and on days when the balloons were flying above low cloud cover the Tiger pilots, safe from observation from the ground, would attempt to bounce their wheels on the tops of them, performing a bizarre aerial trampoline act. All went well until one day a student mis-

calculated and punctured the gasbag with his Tiger's propeller, whereupon the balloon exploded and burnt most of the fabric off the undersides of the Moth. The pilot managed to get back to Fairoaks, suitably chastened. The balloon fell in a fashionable district of Weybridge – and the trampolining ceased.

Although the Tiger Moth's primary role was as a trainer it was a most versatile machine which served in wartime as artillery spotter, light bomber, ground attack aircraft, maritime patroller and even as a remotely-controlled target drone. The Tiger Moth 'bombers' carried eight 25-pound bombs beneath their wings or fuselages. It was this modification which led to the addition of the anti-spin strakes on the rear fuselage which are a feature of most surviving Tigers when it was discovered that with bomb racks fitted the aeroplane was reluctant to recover from a spin. In peacetime the Dutch aviation authorities, evidently a conservative and cautious bunch, demanded an ugly dorsal fin

Left: Appropriate emblem for the famous Tiger Club, based at Redhill Aerodrome in Surrey.

extension on Tigers under their registry for the same reason. Not only is it unnecessary, but it destroyed the distinctive line of de Havilland's fin and rudder.

Another modification involved the fitting of trays under the rear instrument panel in which hand grenades could be stowed. Tiger Moth pilots were supposed to drop the grenades through chutes in the Tiger's floor. But it was the idea that was dropped when pilots pointed out the dangers of a grenade jamming in the chute. Even more absurd was a device called the Paraslasher, invented at the Reid & Sigrist Flying School at Desford, Leicestershire. The Paraslasher was a farmer's hand-scythe attached to an eight foot long pole which projected through the Tiger Moth's lower fuselage and could be swung down for its intended use – cutting the parachute canopies and shroud lines of invading German paratroopers. Reid & Sigrist's chief flying instructor George Lowdell demonstrated it by wheeling around Desford like a demented Dervish, disembowelling straw-stuffed effigies of Hitler and Mussolini. It was never used in action, but at the time a Nazi invasion looked imminent, ploughshares had rapidly to be turned to swords, however makeshift, and it might have worked.

Some Tigers flew without pilots. The D.H.82B Queen Bee which appeared in 1934 was the world's first truly operational pilotless aero-

Left: Evening light catches the wings of a pair of Tiger Moths over Buckinghamshire.

Upper left: The perfect curves of a 'de Havilland' tail, seen here on a D.H.82A Tiger Moth, became a company hallmark, and might well have been inspired by the shape of a moth's wings.

Above: One of nearly 10,000 Mark II Tiger Moths to be built – this one displays a machine-gun mounting – of which some 750 survive.

plane, used as a radio-controlled gunnery target drone. Its guidance system was based on a two-axis autopilot which operated compressed air valves linked to the aircraft's elevators and rudder on command from a radio transmitter. Most of the 420 Queen Bees built were operated on floats for naval gunnery practice and controlled either from a ship's radio room or from a 'portable' console (it stood six feet high and weighed 1,500 pounds) which provided the commands *left, straight, right, climb, level, glide* and *dive* on a telephone-type dial. Radio control was in its infancy then, and Bees were not always cooperative. On one occasion the aircraft's receiver managed to pick up transmissions from a popular radio station, and its resultant flight path was reportedly 'emotioning'. Another tale tells of the time when their Lordships of the Admiralty assembled aboard a fleet of ships in the English Channel to watch a demonstration of naval firepower. The ships poured every kind of fire at the weaving Queen Bee but failed to register a single hit, whereupon the embarrassed

officer organising the show was heard to whisper to the Bee operator 'for heaven's sake dial "Crash"!'

Queen Bees had a rudimentary autoland device triggered by a bob-weight at the end of a trailing aerial. The idea was that when the bob-weight touched the surface of the sea, usually when the Bee was some thirty feet up, it would automatically trigger a 'throttle closed, stick back' command which would flare the aeroplane and allow it to settle gently on the water to await recovery by the mother ship. It worked well enough at sea, but when Bees were adapted for

Top left: Tiger Moth in Royal
Air Force trainer colours –
the alma mater of countless
hundreds of thousands of
pilots the world over.

land use the cluttered approaches to airfields presented too many obstacles to strike the dangling weight, with the inevitable result that land-borne Bees sometimes 'landed' before they were supposed to.

Adaptable in peacetime as in war, the Tiger Moth served in many civilian capacities: as trainer, glider-tug, crop sprayer and airshow performer. In the early 1950s Tigers were plentiful and cheap: my conscience still troubles me that as a child I helped burn a whole pile of them that the local aero club did not want, while recently a Tiger Moth sold for £17,000.

There are about 750 Tiger Moths still in existence. Some are still working aeroplanes earning their livings doing what a Tiger does best: teaching people to fly. Many more have been restored to pristine condition, better even than when they left the factory at Hatfield, or Cowley or the many outposts of Empire where the Tiger's classic form took shape. Few aeroplanes have been held in such affection by different generations as the Tiger. Were they the world's greatest trainers? Those who learned their craft in one would say so. As with first loves, so with first aeroplanes.

A PITTS IS SOME-THING SPECIAL

Curtis Pitts built his first aeroplane in 1932, using the engine from a Model T Ford and such parts as he could find around the family home in Americus, Georgia. It did not fly, which was fortunate, for Pitts was not a pilot, but he did manage to sell the wrecked remains for $6, and with this sum set forth to seek his fortune in Florida. There he went to work for a US Navy aircraft repair yard, and having learned to fly, ran the local airport at St. Augustine. Curtis loved aerobatics, which he performed with a Waco UPF trainer, but he hankered after a machine which would be capable of advanced manoeuvres. The only answer was to design his own, which he did, combining the desirable features of two classic aerobatic biplanes – the Great Lakes from America and the German Bücker Jungmeister.

This original Pitts Special flew for the first time in 1945. It was powered by a 55 hp Lycoming engine 'because it was handy and the money for anything better wasn't', and considering its low power the little Pitts biplane performed remark-ably well. A 90 hp Franklin engine proved even better, and Curtis devised an inverted fuel and oil system for the aeroplane to enlarge its aerobatic repertoire. It was not entirely successful. 'We had inverted fuel problems coming out of our ears,' he recalls, 'and you just never knew whether it was going to work or not. You had to roll over, hold your breath, and pray.' Unfortunately the Florida cropduster to whom Pitts sold the aeroplane was stone deaf. When the inevitable engine failure occurred during a roll he failed to hear the sudden silence up front and the first Pitts Special was wrecked in the ensuing crash.

Around this time Pitts was commissioned to build ten more Specials for Stengels Flying Service in Gainesville. Stengels crashed too, and Pitts found himself the owner of one unfinished Pitts Special aerobatic biplane. This machine, named *Li'l Stinker*, was flown in the famous World Air Shows displays by Pitts' friend and partner Phil Quigley and was later bought by a talented young woman aerobatic pilot, Betty Skelton. In her hands the red and white striped *Li'l Stinker* became a favourite airshow performer on both sides of the Atlantic. Betty Skelton shipped the Pitts to England in 1949 to take part in the *Daily Express* International Air

Over the top: the US Red Devils aerobatic team looping their Pitts S-1S Specials.

Far right: Pitts Specials are popular with amateur builders. This one is a homebuilt S-1C.

Right and below: The Pitts S-2S is a 260 hp single-seat airshow and competition aerobatic aircraft developed from the two-seat S-2A.

Pageant at Gatwick Airport. 'The reaction to *Li'l Stinker* was astounding,' she told reporters later. 'I think it was about the smallest airplane flying at that time, and in England sport flying was expensive. They just fell in love with it.'

In *Li'l Stinker* with its skunk-emblem Betty Skelton took the US Women's Aerobatic title four times in a row between 1948 and 1951. Betty's achievements with the Pitts brought another woman pilot·knocking on Curtis's door: Caro Bayley, who flew a clipwing Piper Cub for World Air Shows, wanted Mr. Pitts to build her one of his little biplanes. This one, named *Black Beauty*, was powered by a 125 hp engine; it was burned out in a fire after a fuel injection line fractured.

The 1950s were bleak times for sport aviation. There was little demand for aerobatic aeroplanes. Curtis and his wife Willie Mae ran a cropdusting business and occasionally sold a set of plans for the Special to homebuilders. With the 1960s came a revival of interest in competition flying and the organisation of the first world aerobatics championships. The World Aeros, as they are popularly known, are scored according to the system devised by José Aresti. There are

US Women's National Aerobatic Champion Mary Gaffaney pictured at the World Aerobatics Championships at RAF Hullavington in 1970 with her Pitts S-1S.

Above left: Bob Herendeen, dean of Pitts' pilots, with his 1970 Pitts S-1S.

Above right: The two-seat Pitts S-2A has proved popular with aerobatics schools and display teams, such as Rothmans, whose founder the late Manx Kelly is seen here inverted against a backdrop of smoke from the three other team members.

some 100,000 possible permutations. Whole sequences can be drawn up like pieces of music, with a difficulty factor assigned to each manoeuvre. Aresti, as already mentioned, placed greatest emphasis, and maximum scoring points, on those manoeuvres performed vertically, with the aircraft either climbing or descending. The clean monoplanes – YAKs and Zlins – favoured by the Eastern Bloc nations dominated the early competitions. The British, French, Spanish and Swiss struggled gamely with elderly Stampe and

Bücker biplanes and the Americans were not even in the running. As for the Pitts Special, which many regarded as a not-too-serious toy, it simply did not seem to be a likely contender, because biplanes are not at their best in the high-scoring vertical figures. Drag from the wings, struts and bracing wires slows them down in the climb, and great power is therefore needed to keep the machine moving upward, though when descending vertically the drag does help prevent excessive speed from building up.

All this time Pitts had been badgered by friends to keep developing his biplane design, and he was watching the European aerobatic pilots with interest. In 1962 he improved the Special design to accommodate engines up to 180 hp. Three years later, and allegedly because of his own spreading waistline, he enlarged the cockpit, and in 1966 made what was perhaps the most significant improvement of all when he designed a set of symmetrical airfoil wings for the aircraft. In fact Curtis Pitts had been experimenting with symmetrical wing sections for years, with airshow work rather than outright competition aerobatics in mind. 'We didn't like the first wings worth a hoot,' he told *Sport Aviation* magazine, 'so we tore them down and modified them, put them back on again, tore 'em down again.' So it went on until the definitive wing design appeared in 1967, with four ailerons to improve the aircraft's roll rate. Pitts used two different airfoil sections for the upper and lower wings. The design was patented, and only Pitts himself would supply sets of custom-built symmetrical section wings to approved customers.

One such was a Trans World Airlines pilot named Bob Herendeen, who acquired the second set of wings built by Pitts for his homebuilt aeroplane. In 1966 Herendeen took part in his first World Championships. He placed twenty-fifth, while at Magdeburg, East Germany two years later he worked his way up to third. Then in the summer of 1970, Herendeen and the Pitts burst onto the international aerobatics scene at RAF Hullavington in Wiltshire, England. Herendeen and four other members of the United States team were flying finely-tuned 180 hp Pitts Specials. Although a Russian won the contest it was the Specials which captured the hearts of spectators and judges alike. They seemed so absurdly *tiny*, spanning just 17 feet. Standing alongside the cockpit a man could nearly stretch out to the wingtip. But the Pitts' climb rate, its 180-degree per second roll, and ability to perform mind-boggling snap manoeuvres in breathless succession was astonishing. It was a cheeky, snappy insect of an aeroplane compared to the slow, graceful Russian YAKs. One observer noted that the YAK was 'the grand piano' of aerobatic aircraft. If so, I submit that a Pitts is the xylophone. The Russian pilots flew a Pitts, and one of them concluded, grudgingly: 'Good aeroplane for fun. Not good for contests.' He placed eighteenth, Bob Herendeen came second.

Two years later when the World Aerobatic Championships were held at Salon de Provence in France the American team's Pitts Specials took team and individual men's and women's trophies, and 'Pa' Pitts was rewarded with a ceremonial ducking in the team's hotel's swimming pool for his part in giving America its first ever victory in the Olympics of competition aerobatic flying.

Newer designs have since emerged which are better suited to the esoteric demands of unlimited class aerobatics, but the Pitts Special remains the dream of any aspiring aerobaticist. It has a certain charisma which the modern monoplanes lack. Evolved over a protracted gestation period, a Pitts is a near perfect aeroplane for the pilot who wants to spend as little time as possible right side up. The airframe is immensely strong, stressed to +9g and −4½g, so that it is very difficult to break, indeed I know of no Pitts Special built the way that Curtis intended that has come apart in the air, though the constant

Below: The two-seat Pitts S-2A has proved a popular mount with formation aerobatic teams. Right: The late Neil Williams, thirteen times British Aerobatic Champion, in knife-edge flight with a Pitts S-1S.

Above: Jordan's Royal Falcons aerobatic team fly Pitts S-2As.

Above right: A Pitts S-1S.

Right: Formation roll with two erect, two inverted from Rothman's Aerobatic Team.

punishment of aerobatics takes its toll in fatigue on the welded tube fuselage structure. Some competition Specials are on their third or fourth fuselages. With the 180 or 200 hp engines used on the Pitts S-1S and S-1T models (which are factory- as opposed to home-built), and an empty weight of just 1,150 pounds, a Pitts has an excellent power-to-weight ratio for vertical manoeuvres.

I have seen Bob Herendeen take an S-1T through a vertical snap roll, four-point hesitation vertical roll and a three-and-a-half turn torque roll (in which the aeroplane falls vertically backwards, rotating under engine torque) in quick succession, and cap it off with a 16-turn inverted flat spin which had everyone holding their breath for far too long. The short span wings and four ailerons provide rates of roll the like of which can rotate your stomach through 360 degrees before your head knows it has gone! The climb rate – either way up thanks to Curtis's symmetrical section wings – is in the order of 2,600 feet per minute. Most endearing of all the Pitts' qualities is its control response and harmony. The ailerons are feather-light and frictionless. On my first ride in a Pitts (a two-seat S-2A, which Pitts first flew in 1966 and which was put into production in 1971, the first open-cockpit biplane certificated in the United States since the 1930s) I was handed the stick to try for myself and having pushed it firmly to one side of the

cockpit to make what I supposed would be a moderate rate turn, found myself half way through a second aileron roll before I knew what had happened, and on top of a rich curry lunch thoughtfully provided by the Pitts' owners. Fortunately the absence of an intercom between cockpits spared me the wrath of my companion.

Such is the response of a well-rigged Pitts that it tends to inflate the ego of a would-be aerobatic pilot. Curtis Pitts is quick to caution homebuilders of his design against over-confidence, which can easily flatter a not especially competent flier into some act of foolishness. What happens in a Pitts happens very quickly, and it is vital to keep mentally ahead of the aeroplane. In skilled hands a Pitts will perform virtually any manoeuvre you can call to mind, and more than a few that you might rather not. It has faults – poor pilot visibility when landing, and perhaps it is a trifle too small to be seen properly from the ground when performing at the heights used in unlimited aerobatic competition – but no red-blooded pilot can resist a quickening of the pulse at the sight of a sunburst striped Pitts, nor is there one who would not sell his soul for the chance to fly one. Even Curtis Pitts himself, who might be forgiven for feeling blase about the little biplane which he has honed to a fine edge in more than 30 years, admits that his first flight in the original Special was his biggest thrill. Quite simply, a Pitts Special is *very* special.

MOUNT OF ACES

Every little while I crash a Camel,
Every little while I hit a tree;
I'm always stalling, always falling,
Because I want to fly a posh S.E.

The 'posh S.E.' was the S.E.5A, a product of the government-owned Royal Aircraft Factory at Farnborough, whose record of aircraft design in the early years of the First World War was scarcely encouraging and perhaps best remembered (or forgotten, depending on your point of view) for the dismal R.E.8 'Harry Tate' reconnaissance aircraft introduced late in 1916 and universally despised by Royal Flying Corps pilots. There was no lack of design and engineering talent at Farnborough, but it was directed towards outdated concepts by an empire building civil servant named Mervyn O'Gorman who was the Royal Aircraft Factory's superintendent, a man dedicated to ensuring that if Farnborough

could not produce aeroplanes to rival those which Germany had, no private enterprise manufacturer would get the chance. Fortunately he failed in his goal.

Against this unpromising background a design team led by H. P. 'Harry' Folland began work in 1916 on a new scout, centred on the aluminium monobloc Hispano-Suiza 8A V-8 engine, which put out 150 hp and was free of the problems which rotary engines created for inexperienced pilots: it had a progressive throttle for smooth control of power, and there were no gyroscopic forces to take into account. Folland's aim was to design a compact and rugged biplane which could be flown safely by pilots of limited experience (at the time pilots were arriving at the Front with fewer than 20 hours' total flying time), and which would be stable enough to provide a steady gun platform, the opposite approach to that which produced the agile Sopwith scouts.

The prototype S.E.5 (S.E. stood for Scout, Experimental) was completed on 20 November 1916 and first flew two days later in the hands of Major F. W. Gooden. On 4 January 1917 Gooden took the aeroplane up for a short test and it broke up in the air; the wings failed because some wooden webs had been omitted from the drawings. Two months later the first production S.E.5s were delivered to Martlesham Heath for

Below: The S.E.5A's upper wing Lewis gun armament is evident in this view of the Shuttleworth Trust's machine.

Right: Front view of the Shuttleworth Trust's S.E.5A shows blunt and businesslike appearance of H. P. Folland's rugged and compact design.

testing by service pilots. Their report was not encouraging, pointing out the S.E.5's poor lateral control, lack of manoeuvrability, indifferent slow speed handling and the inadequacy of the huge 'glasshouse' windscreen which swept around the cockpit sides and seriously hampered the pilot's vision, especially during landing.

Such had been the compressed timetable of the S.E.5's design, development and production that it was too late to make any radical changes. The first production aircraft were already in the hands of 56 Squadron, Royal Flying Corps at London Colney, where a hand-picked team of experienced pilots were flying the new scout. Among them was Albert Ball, who was to score 44 recorded victories in the war and was posthumously awarded the Victoria Cross. Ball had been flying the nimble Nieuport 17, and he did not take to the S.E.5. He wrote home: 'They have put me on an S.E.5 machine but I should like to get back to my old machine as soon as possible. Oh, I shall never be able to do my job, I must fly another machine . . . The S.E.5 has turned out to be a dud. It's speed is only about half Nieuport speed *(not true, the S.E.5 and Nieuport 17 were closely matched for speed, and later S.E.s were faster than the French machine)* . . . It is such a great shame, for everybody thinks they are so good and expects such a lot from them.'

Ball made a number of changes in an effort to tune his S.E. to his needs (and kept a Nieuport in reserve). Away went the glasshouse windscreen, which some pilots replaced with a tiny aero screen from the Avro 504, though Ball dispensed with his entirely, and he also lowered his seating position and – according to some sources – removed the fuselage-mounted Vickers machine-gun, which on the S.E.5 was one of the first installations to employ the Constantinesco interrupter gear mechanism for firing between the revolving blades of the propeller. The Vickers was prone to jamming and plagued with synchronisation problems on the early S.E.s. Ball reputedly favoured the Lewis gun mounted on a Foster rack on top of the upper wing centre section, although this installation, with its drum-fed ammunition, was difficult to reload.

Back at Farnborough, meanwhile, the third prototype S.E.5 had been modified to accept the 200 hp geared Hispano-Suiza 8B engine, and became the much improved S.E.5A, which was also built with 220 hp Hissos, and 200 hp Wolseley Viper and Adder engines. As experience was gained on the S.E. it became apparent that much of the initial resistance to the aeroplane stemmed from pilots' background on highly-manoeuvrable rotary-engined aircraft, which were ideally suited to skilled fliers. The S.E.5 was an entirely different concept, an aeroplane which was tolerant and forgiving, could give a modestly skilled pilot a reasonable chance of hitting something in a dogfight and was a rock-steady gun

'Warm, comfortable, an easy machine to fly', reported James McCudden, who scored 51 of his 57 victories with S.E.5As.

platform on which the talented marksman could capitalise. It still had faults: the early licence-built Hisso engines were of poor quality and prone to sudden failure, and the aeroplane suffered badly from adverse yaw in turns, but it was predictable and would never bite a careless hand as quickly or as finally as would the Sopwith Camel. Each, in its way, helped establish Allied air superiority in the final years of the war. And, unexpectedly after its inauspicious beginnings, it was the S.E.5 which was the 'mount' of Britain's best-known aces.

Albert Ball scored 13 of his 44 victories with an S.E.5 in a period of 12 days in late April and early May 1917. At 5.30 pm on the evening of 7 May he took off from Vert Galand airfield, leading ten other S.E.5s on an offensive sweep in the Cambrai-Douai area, and subsequently clashed with Albatros D-IIIs from Manfred von Richthofen's *Jagdstaffel II*, led in the *Staffelführer*'s absence by his younger brother Lothar. The weather deteriorated and some three hours later Ball, leader of 56 Squadron A Flight, and Captain C. M. Crowe, commander of B Flight, met up over the village of Fresnoy and engaged a solitary Albatros. Lothar von Richthofen was at the controls. What happened next remains open to question, but it appears that Ball damaged the fleeing Albatros, which crash-landed leaving von Richthofen uninjured. Witnesses on the ground reported that Ball's S.E.5 disappeared into cloud

and then re-appeared inverted trailing oil smoke, to crash near the village of Annoeullin. Ball died within seconds, though his only injuries were those sustained in the crash. Nor was there substantial evidence of the S.E.5 having taken mortal fire, though Lothar von Richthofen was officially credited with the victory. Perhaps, exhausted after long hours of combat duty, Ball simply became disorientated in cloud and lost control of his machine.

There is controversy also over the death of another great S.E.5 exponent, Major Edward 'Mick' Mannock. 'Mick', popularly styled 'The King of the Air Fighters', developed a deep hatred of Germans when he was imprisoned in appalling conditions by German sympathisers in Turkey at the outbreak of the First World War, prompting him to join the Army on his return to England with the intention of 'killing as many of the swine as possible'. A cocky, self-opinionated youngster, his early service with the Royal Flying Corps earned him a reputation as a naive and brash braggart, but he matured into a single-minded fighter whose skills as a marksman are legendary (and were not, as those legends so often have it, attributable to his having only one eye. His left eye was *weakened* by a childhood infection, but functioned). Mannock, who developed a maudlin fear of burning to death after seeing one of his early victims go down in flames, died on 26 July 1918 when his S.E.5A, apparent-

Though it lacked the temperamental agility of some rotary-engined scouts, the S.E.5A was a rock-steady gun platform which provided a modestly skilled pilot with a reasonable chance of hitting something.

Shuttleworth Trust's S.E.5A.

ly hit by groundfire, crashed near the village of La Pierre-au-Beure while he was on patrol with a new and inexperienced pilot. His body was apparently buried near the scene but, though the S.E.5A burned on impact, it was unmarked. One theory is that in fear of the end he dreaded most, 'Mick' Mannock leapt from the crashing biplane at the last moment.

James McCudden, who joined the Royal Flying Corps in 1913 as an air mechanic, flew an S.E.5 for the first time while attached to 56 Squadron in France after a spell at home as a flying instructor. He never flew another type thereafter, using his skill as a mechanic to improve and hone his S.E.5 to a fine edge with which he claimed 51 of his 57 victims. McCudden died, not in combat, but as the result of an uncharacteristic mistake. While returning to France from leave to take command of 60 Squadron his S.E.5A's engine failed on take-off, and the machine stalled and crashed when he tried to turn back towards the airfield. Let his words on the S.E.5A be its epitaph, too: 'It was a warm, comfortable and easy machine to fly'.

FRIENDLY DRAGONS

Edward Hillman's brief was simple: 'Build me a Moth with two engines and room for up to eight passengers'. The de Havilland company's response was equally succinct. They showed him designer Arthur Hagg's drawings for the D.H.84 Dragon, drawn up at the request of the Iraqi Air Force. 'I'll take four', said Hillman.

Hillman was the owner of a road haulage company who had started an airline service between his base at Maylands, near Romford in Essex and the towns of Clacton and Ramsgate, using D.H.83 Fox Moths. He wanted a twin-engine machine for a planned cut-price service to Paris. Within two months Hubert Broad took the prototype Dragon into the air from Stag Lane, and a week later, in December 1932, freshly painted in Hillman's blue and white livery, it was delivered to Maylands, where Amy Johnson waited to christen it. Hillman had three of his four Dragons by 1 April 1933 when the Paris service was inaugurated, and had ordered two more.

'Superficially there is little to tell one that the new Dragon is a very remarkable aircraft,' reported a contemporary aviation magazine. It was true enough. The Dragon was an unimposing looking biplane with a slabsided plywood fuselage, a pair of 130 hp Gipsy Major 1 engines, and Gipsy Moth outer wing panels fitted with new tapered ailerons. But it *was* a remarkable machine, for with a standard load of six passengers and their luggage it cruised at 109 mph and burned a paltry 13 gallons of fuel per hour — more economical than the four-passenger single-engined Fox Moth. Hillman was able to offer flights to Paris for £3. 15s. 0d. single, £6 return, while his rivals Imperial Airways and Air France were charging £5 and £8 for the same journeys.

The Dragon, which began as a short-run custom built machine for Hillman, was soon in great demand by the numerous small airlines which proliferated around Britain in the 1930s, and was instrumental in opening up routes to the Western Isles of Scotland and to the Channel Islands, where Jersey Airways' Dragons were a

popular tourist attraction operating off the sandy beach at Jersey's St. Aubin's Bay before the island's airport was built. Between 1933 and 1935 115 Dragons were built in Britain; a further 87 were manufactured in Australia during the Second World War as radio and navigation trainers for the Royal Australian Air Force.

The success of the Dragon brought de Havillands an order from the Australian Government for a four-engined biplane airliner to serve the Singapore-Australia sector of the new England-Australia airmail route. This was the D.H.86 whose elegant airframe inspired a further twin-engined biplane to replace the Dragon – the D.H.89 Dragon Six, which, as its name suggested, was powered by the 200 hp six-cylinder Gipsy Six engine. The prototype flew for the first time on 17 April 1934, and during early trials reached a maximum speed of 175 mph, whereupon the nose buckled. A speed restriction of 160 mph was imposed, with cruising speed around 135 mph, which was a great improvement on the Dragon. The prototype was sold to a Swiss operator. Edward Hillman bought the first production aircraft, which Hubert Broad flew in the 1934 King's Cup Air Race on 13 July, averaging a commendable 158 mph before hail damage to the Dragon Six's wings forced him to retire.

Above: One of the world's most attractive biplanes, the de Havilland D.H.90 Dragonfly.

A pair of visiting Dragonflies at
Old Warden airfield.

Dragon Rapide cabin.

D.H.86 Express cockpit.

D.H.90 Dragonfly.

Top: Float-equipped D.H.84 Dragon operating in Canada.

Above: Dragon Rapides formed the backbone of Britain's pre- and post-war feeder airline services. This one operated from Blackpool Airport.

A special stripped down Dragon Six was built for the 1934 MacRobertson Mildenhall-Melbourne air race. Named *Tainui* after the first Maori war canoe to reach New Zealand, and flown by Squadron Leader J. D. Hewett and C. E. Kay, the Dragon Six reached Australia after a total of 106 hours, 51 minutes and 28 seconds flying time, placing sixth in the handicap section of that famous race, and fifth in the speed event.

Though officially known in those early days as the Dragon Six, the D.H.89 was soon renamed Dragon Rapide. Between 1934-1946 727 were built at the de Havilland factory at Hatfield and by the Brush Coachworks company at Loughborough, which manufactured most of the aircraft delivered to the Royal Air Force during the Second World War as Dominie navigation trainers and communications aircraft. Surplus Dominies and Rapides were the corner stone of many post-war airlines. One of the largest fleets was that of British European Airways, which operated 18 Rapides on its Scottish, Scilly and Channel Islands routes. A handful of Dragon Rapides still survive, in the hands of private owners who cherish them as they never were in workaday service. One gives summer joy-rides in

the south of England, operating from the same airfields which Rapides served with the airlines as recently as 20 years ago.

There is a third Dragon which should be mentioned, one which I place very near the top of any list of the world's most attractive aeroplanes: the D.H.90 Dragonfly. Although it resembled a smaller Rapide, the five-seat Dragonfly incorporated the pre-formed plywood monocoque construction used on the de Havilland Comet racer and Albatross airliner (two more beauties). Its slightly swept wings were a masterpiece of styling, relatively free of the encumbrance of struts

and wire bracing, the two Gipsy Major engines housed in typical DH fashion with 'trousered' undercarriage legs. This Dragonfly first appeared in August 1935, a business aircraft, highly priced at £2,650 whose first customers included Lord Beaverbrook, Sir Philip Sassoon and Loel Guinness. Sixty-six were built, but the complexities of repairing and renovating the three-ply moulded monocoque have ensured that few survived. The only airworthy example was restored to factory-new condition in England in 1981, at heaven knows what cost. Whatever it may have been, it was worth it!

Top: Military Rapides were known as Dominies and served as navigation and wireless telegraphy trainers and communications aircraft with the Royal Air Force and Royal Navy.

Above: The D.H.86 four-engined airliner was designed for the Australian Government for the Singapore-Australia air mail route. This Quantas D.H.86 was photographed at Darwin.

A PORTFOLIO OF BIPLANES

VICKERS-VIMY-ROLLS.

THE FIRST DIRECT FLIGHT ACROSS THE ATLANTIC.
JUNE.14-15.1919.
CAPT: SIR JOHN ALCOCK K.B.E. D.S.C.-PILOT.
LIEUT: SIR ARTHUR WHITTEN BROWN K.B.E.-NAVIGATOR.

The Vickers Vimy, designed as a bomber, was the vehicle for many pioneering flights, including the first flight from England to Australia by Ross and Keith Smith, and Sir John Alcock and Sir Arthur Whitten Brown's epic first non-stop aerial crossing of the Atlantic Ocean in 1919.

Top left: A contemporary of the Handley Page H.P.42 was the Short Scylla, a 39-passenger landplane development of Imperial Airways' Short Scipio flying boats.

Above: The Boeing P-12 pursuit fighter was Boeing's first combat aircraft and was widely used by the US Army and US Navy (as the F4B) in the inter-war period.

Far left: This Curtiss F9C-2 Sparrowhawk was one of seven 'parasite' fighters operated experimentally from the US Navy airships Akron and Macon. The hook mounted atop the upper wing enabled the aircraft to engage a trapeze suspended below the airships' bellies in flight.

Left: Jimmy Doolittle pictured with the Vought 02U-1 Corsair biplane in which he conducted blind flying trials for the Guggenheim Flight Laboratory.

The Great Lakes Trainer 2T-1A was first put into production in 1929. One of the classic American biplane designs it has several times been revived. The Great Lakes pictured here is a late 1970s model.

Smoke on, go! Stampe
SV-4Bs of the Rothmans
Aerobatic Team
photographed in 1971.

Above: Biplanes are still in production. This one is a Schweizer AgCat agricultural aircraft powered by a 450 hp Pratt & Whitney Wasp Junior engine.

Top right: The Whing Ding ultralight was designed by Californian Robert Hovey as a simple-to-construct homebuilt fun machine. It is powered by a 14 hp two-stroke engine.

Far right: Farman Goliath airliner used by Air France's forerunner Air Union.

Right: 'Comfort on board the French plane Farman Goliath', says the original caption. The Goliath was used by Air Union for London-Paris services carrying 12 passengers (in wicker armchairs) between the two capitals in a little under three hours.

A more sophisticated homebuilt biplane is the fully-aerobatic two-seat cabin Sorrell Hiperbipe. Note negative stagger wings and untapered airfoil-section fuselage providing additional lift for knife-edge flight.

Right and centre right: The Belgian-designed Stampe SV-4, a contemporary of the Tiger Moth and Bücker Jungmann, was mass-produced in France as a civil and military two-seat trainer and is still found in small numbers at flying clubs and with private owners.

The Stits Sky Baby was the world's smallest aeroplane. It was built in 1952 by Californian Ray Stits and had tiny biplane wings spanning just 7 feet 2 inches. It was powered by a 112 hp Continental engine and flew at nearly 200 mph. The Sky Baby is preserved in the Experimental Aircraft Association's museum in Wisconsin.

INDEX

ACKNOWLEDGMENTS

Picture Credits

The majority of the illustrations in
this book have been selected from
the author's own collection. For the
remaining photographs we would
like to thank the following for their
kind assistance.
Air France – pp 186 (bottom), 187
(bottom)

Air Portraits – pp 98/99
ALIA Royal Jordanian Airline – pp
164 (top)
Beech Aircraft Corp – pp 60/61 (all
6), 63 (bottom), 64/65 (all 5)
Boeing Aircraft Corp, Wichita – pp
76 (both), 77 (both)
British Aerospace – pp 93 (inset),
96/97 (both), 112/113, 116/117
(both), 166/167 (all 4), 178 (both),

179
British Airways – pp 52/53 (both), 54
(both), 56/57, 124 (bottom), 182 (top)
Canadian National Aeronautical
Collection – pp 28/29
Don Blackburn – pp 24 (inset)
Don Dwiggins, pp 187 (top)
Great Lakes Aircraft Company – pp
184 (inset)
Gulf Oil Corporation – pp 132,

132/133
Ray Russell – pp 32/33, 38/39
Sikorsky pp 86/87 (all 3), 88/89 (all
3)
Smithsonian Institute – pp 11, 12/13
(both)
U.S. Navy – pp 20/21, 20 (both),
128/129, 130/131 (both), 182
(bottom)
Vickers Ltd. – pp 180/181 (both)